# How to Be a God

## Volume One: Sex With Humans
### (The Science of Living Right)

## *Saint Sierra*

Writers Club Press
San Jose  New York  Lincoln  Shanghai

How to Be a God
Volume One: Sex With Humans
(The Science of Living Right)

Writers Club Press
an imprint of iUniverse.com, Inc.

For information address:
iUniverse.com, Inc.
5220 S 16th, Ste. 200
Lincoln, NE 68512
www.iuniverse.com

ISBN: 0-595-00156-4

Printed in the United States of America

*for
Charity
and
Generosity*

# ∾Contents∾

# ∾Acknowledgments∾

*Of the many teachers I have had,*

*two in particular deserve special thanks.*

*Elaine Morgan,*

*who helped me begin to understand where we've been;*

*and F. Paul Wilson,*

*who showed me where we might go.*


*Their books are listed first and second in the Appendix*

*at the back of this manual.*

*Please buy them and read them frequently.*

*Buy several copies, to give to friends.*

*They will thank you.*

Opening Testament:
# Keep Your Fucking Hands Off

~Book One~

# Genocide

# ❧Chapter 1❧

1. And the gods came to know of life, and joy; and they wanted more.

2. And we gave many forms to life, and one of the stories took place on the third planet of a small star; and the way that we became you is thus:

3. On a whirling dust mote tossed into space, the gods created the human race.

4. As the planet slowed and cooled, we began to seed it with life. And the more of ourselves we put into the planet, the more life grew.

5. And we are still learning to be that life.

6. This is the story, then, of how we on Earth came to have life; the mistakes we have made, and what they mean; and where you are going.

7. Life grows always in tiny steps. Tiny life began to grow in the waters: they learned to grow bigger, and to become different kinds of life.

8. And their beauty and variety were great, but not enough; so some went to the edge, and ventured forth, and became even greater.

9. Some did not make the leap all the way. They stayed on the edge and are yet so. Those who could not choose between one or the other became amphibians.

10. Crossing the barrier between water and land became a vital tool for the shaping of a species, one that we would use again.

11. The life on the land went in many more diverse directions than it had in the water. Some life grew green and stayed put. Some grew legs and walked....

12. Each molecule is life, and ever reaches for life: never forget that the twin drives of any organism are to survive and to reproduce.

13. So the molecules multiplied, and became the wind and the restless waves. The green life grew, and the life that walked grew ever more varied. And life continued to reach for life.

14. Life is change.

15. Many species are born each day from change. Those that change in ways that tend to foster survival are more likely to live long enough to breed. Those that do not adapt to changing circumstances die out.

16. In this way came to be human beings. The changes that shaped humans and the echoes therefrom which have multiplied down the millennia shall be herein explained.

17. They walked and climbed and ate fruit; and life was good. There were males and females and children: there was sun and water and fresh air; and life was good.

18. But then the weather changed. And changed, and changed, and changed.

19. And the world began to change, and life became hard.

20. There were a great many creatures living in the trees. But it began to be hot, and the trees began to die. It grew hotter, and the forest began to die. Everywhere, the world began to dry up and die.

21. The smallest creatures learned to climb higher in the trees. There was food there, and safety from the larger creatures.

22. The larger creatures grew even larger and became the best at competing for food on the ground.

23. The creatures in the middle had no place to go; for their world had begun to reject them. Mankind has not yet forgiven his world.

24. There was no room in the trees, and no food or safety on the ground.

25. But there was the water.

26. The creatures in the middle had nowhere to go. All the good food, except for insects and such, was in the trees. The water holes that had not dried up were being hogged by large carnivores, who were

likely to chase and maybe eat, these poor middle-sized orphans.

27. Thus the mother of all humans was born. Hungry, thirsty, tired from carrying her baby: when the lion came charging at her, she ran straight into the sea.

# ∼Chapter 2∽

1. The human race grew from survivors able to adapt to change.

2. The first big change was the weather, which forced her out of her home. The next change came when she took a risk.

3. The risk paid off. She wasn't eaten by the lion like her sister, nor did she die of thirst like her aunt. Her children neither died nor fell from the womb.

4. She ran into the ocean to escape the lion. Since she could stand upright, the carnivore could not follow her: it grew tired of waiting and went in search of dry prey.

5. So there was safety in the water; and crabs and shrimp that were like the insects she was used to eating, and eggs from seabirds; and streams coming down to the sea for her fresh water.

6. There was even relief from the heat, and life should have been good.

7.  But any organism undergoing such a radical change in their environment will inevitably also themselves change: again we used the barrier between water and land to shape a species.

8.  She had to stand up in the water, to keep from drowning herself or her baby; but it was kind of fun, and she began to stand up in shallower water, and finally on land.

9.  And there were many other changes going on.

10. She lost her fur, of course. It didn't keep her warm in the water, and wet fur is cold on land.

11. She grew instead a layer of fat; here, there, and everywhere.

12. She grew some on her lips, so that she could keep her mouth closed under water; and they grew to be most kissable.

13. She grew some to pad her bottom so she could sit on the beach.

14. She grew larger as do all animals that go back into the water, such as dolphins and whales. Her legs became longer and straighter; and grew closer together, for she now spent her time swimming and walking instead of scrambling through the trees.

15. And there were more changes coming, because her baby was so hard to nurse in the water.

16. Having that new padding to sit on was nice, but the silly baby kept falling off the spigot. The baby

couldn't hang on to wet skin the way he had hung on to her fur. And it made her arms so tired to keep holding him up. How to feed baby without getting a permanent backache?

17. She grew breasts.

18. Large, pendulous breasts, shaped as handfuls, solved that particular problem. But sitting on the sand so much brought still other problems.

19. Her tender genitals quickly tired of being ground into the sand and stones. All the remarkable changes in the visible human anatomy have not, combined, shaped the evolution, history, and shape of humanity as much as this single, minor migration. Her love nest went into hiding.

20. Keep in mind that all these changes resulted in enhanced survival, and obviously keeping her genitals safe from abrasion, infection, and hungry fish had an evolutionary benefit.

21. But that's all the damn good it did!

22. Evolution moved the vaginal entrance down and in; put it safely between the woman's firm, strong legs.

23. And men have never forgiven them.

# ∿Chapter 3∿

1. Evolution does not select for the organism's dignity, pleasure, or peace of mind. Evolution selects for survival.

2. It is not necessary that there be happiness; only fatherhood is needed for the human race to continue. This is why women need to be capable of so much more forgiveness than men:

3. The poor guy couldn't reach it anymore.

4. So he had to do something about it.

5. Man's penis was adapted to a straight entry from the rear. But the target was moving steadily away from him.

6. His penis grew larger, and is by far the largest one among the primates. But he couldn't teach it to turn corners. Question: What was he to do?

7. Answer. He invented rape.

8. She kept trying to do it the way they always had, but it wasn't working for him. He got frustrated and blamed her. And some bright ancestor to the toolmakers

guessed it might work better from the other direction, so he threw her on her back and rammed it in.

9. And thus the father of man was born, for he had learned three things.

10. He had learned to commit unprovoked violence against a member of his own species.

11. He found that violence brought pleasure.

12. And he learned to link violence with sex.

13. The species was undergoing a sexual crisis and would have died out. It remains to be seen if that was less drastic than the solution: becoming the species that specializes in violence against its own.

14. All of the pain and despair in life can be traced eventually to this event. In order to survive they had to learn how to hurt each other.

15. Those that survived were the men who could be brutal enough. They passed those genes on. The women who survived would be those that required the least amount of violence. They also bred and passed their genes on. Evolution has bred for aggressive men and submissive women.

16. And men and women may never again understand each other, or trust each other. Or even like each other.

17. Becoming human has been a glorious adventure, and the tragic aftereffect of just the war between the sexes has been a high price to pay. But the real horrors of humanity have come from real war.

# ~Chapter 4~

1. The first weapon was invented by a child.

2. Tossing a pebble at a rock, a playmate, a crab—Hey! Look, you guys! I killed a crab with this rock!—and the idea of death from a distance was born.

3. Killing food with weapons quickly caught on with kids and adults alike. It was surer, safer, and a heck of a lot more fun.

4. Unfortunately man soon found bashing his brother far more rewarding than simply doing in his dinner.

5. Since one man can keep five hundred women continuously pregnant, that makes *499* excess for every one you need. One of the functions of war is occupying and entertaining the excess men.

6. The main reason for war is maximizing genetic variation. The drive for war comes from deep within a society, and comes long before the justifications of politicians and pundits.

7. War cannot exist without a border. This is so whether the border is one of centuries and based on

a natural feature, or was delineated yesterday by a group of rebels. A civil war is no exception, consisting of two or more groups fighting for control of the territory within a border.

8.  A border encloses a limited gene pool within an artificial boundary. But the drive of life reaching for life will overcome any barrier; and the tighter the confinement, the more violent must be the eventual eruption.

9.  A war is the movement of a large number of men into a different gene pool. The one inevitable end product of any armed conflict is a large group of women and children who must depend on men from another gene pool for their survival.

10. Rape is not an unfortunate byproduct of war. It is the reason for war.

11. If there is to be a way for humans to stop hurting each other so much, it will of necessity begin with the recognition of why men really fight.

12. The phrase "man's inhumanity to man" is a contradiction in terms, for it was only the acquisition of the capacity to be inhuman which unleashed the potential that was to blossom into the human race.

13. They had to learn death in order to live.

# ～Chapter 5～

1. We have not thus far painted a very pretty picture of humanity, but it gets worse.

2. However, it also gets better.

3. The missing link is going to remain missing; for too much of the critical development took place at the shore. The bones that carry the clues were long ago washed out to sea.

4. But you can do some digging in your own soul, using the hints you find in your society.

5. You are the orphans of the universe: knocked around more than any species that has survived. You have come into the world with a lot of bruises.

6. But that is *no* excuse.

## ~Book Two~

# Above All Else, KYFHO

# ∿Chapter 1∿

1. Absolute personal responsibility is the only state of mind acceptable for a human being.

2. From this practice will grow self esteem.

3. Children should begin firearm safety and self defense training before they begin school. This would, within a generation, eliminate all trace of the vermin who prey on the innocent.

4. Give no quarter to those who whine and grovel and snivel. Turn only the back of your hand to scapegoat religions. The mark of a human is how tall they can stand, not how low they can go.

5. The creation of a border is invariably accompanied by the imposition of a 'government.' This is a mechanism designed to benefit the greedy and unscrupulous few at the expense of the many.

6. There is no such thing as the state. There are only individuals. It is never acceptable to force sacrifice on a minority, even a minority of one, to further a group-generated aim. There is no goal worthy enough to ever justify the initiation of force.

7.  Without hesitation, use all force necessary for self defense. The gravest sin is the initiation of violence against another.

8.  Every adult has an absolute duty to self and society to stop such violence; and to prevent, as much as is possible, any recurrence.

9.  Each adult needs to acquire lifelong habits: self control and discipline; weapon skills and self defense, and acting with love and honor toward one's self and one's community.

10. From the above guidelines will come self esteem and self respect. Trust yourself, believe in yourself, and do the best you can.

11. Never stop trying to do better.

12. Accept that you are not perfect, and will usually fall short of your goals. Set your goals so that you can achieve them: small and simple and easy to reach. Each small victory will bring confidence and pride.

13. These things alone will bring liberty, and justice, for ALL.

14. Freedom is not the right to do as you choose. Freedom is the ability to choose to do right.

15. Freedom makes people strong, proud, and brave. Free people do not need to be ruled, for they rule themselves. Those who wish to govern do not wish people to be free. It is much easier to rule ignorant, frightened, guilty people.

16. Mankind long ago traded their freedom for government.

17. There are secondary enslavements such as religion, medicine, and the education industry; and these have caused grief enough. But the universal misery the world suffers from is imposed largely by governments.

18. A free person takes pride in solving their own problems without looking to the government for a hand to hold or a handout. They do not need to justify their existence through being needed by parasites.

# ∾Chapter 2∾

1. The desire to control the lives of others is the most destructive and corrosive hangover from man's unfortunate heritage.

2. Reserve your utmost contempt for those that would impose their will on you 'for your own good.' Given sufficient information, you can always make the best choice for yourself. Trust your own judgment.

3. Government is a mechanism with two functions. It takes money by force from those that produce it, for the benefit of the governors. And it uses whatever money is left to keep itself in power.

4. Eliminating these parasites will be painful for them, whether it is done quickly or slowly. The rest of the populace will suffer less if it is done quickly.

5. Government will be eliminated as soon as each person can govern themselves.

6. Self reliance, self respect, and self control are the recipe for doing away with parasites.

7.   A free and informed populace can neither be placed in, nor held in, bondage for longer than they choose; but people can not decide en masse to be free. It is an aggregate of personal decisions, made one person at a time.

8.   The decision to take responsibility for your life will have benefits which only begin with shedding the yoke of government.

9.   Acting with the certainty that you are doing what is right brings you the joy of feeling close to the gods.

10.  KYFHO is a philosophy of love and joy. It is the belief in the absolute right of the individual to live in complete reliance on themself, asking no permissions and causing no harm.

11.  KYFHO is the belief that no person has the right to initiate violence against another.

12.  It is the belief that each person has the potential to govern their own actions better than any outside agency can; and that given the chance, they will.

13.  It is the belief that the best thing you can do for yourself and those around you is to do the best that you can do.

14.  KYFHO is the voice of the gods within you, teaching you how to be the best human you can be.

The KYFHO Commandments:

~Book Three~

# ReDefinition

# ∽Chapter 1∽

1.  And the truth shall set you free…but first it will piss you off.

2.  Ignorance is not bliss.

3.  Ignorance is squalor and misery and disease and despair. Keeping the people ignorant is a primary tool, of any government, for oppression and control. This is also true of any oppression-based agency.

4.  Making knowledge a sin keeps the power in the hands of the ruling class of the Church. Keeping knowledge of medicine and law in the hands of the practitioners thereof, is to place much wealth and power in those same hands.

5.  The more power you grant to oppressive agencies, the more you abdicate responsibility for your own life.

6.  A very wise man has observed the fact that not only do the government, the media, and big business not tell the truth; they do, rather, tell the exact opposite of the truth. Issuing a denial is a dead giveaway every time.

7. And it is a fact of your life that all of the aforementioned agencies **do** in fact tell you a good many things, and all for your own good.

8. Therefore it is wise to distrust everything said by anyone employed in any of the following industries:
   Government
   Medicine
   Law & Justice
   Religion
   Education
   Advertising

9. Learning to hear what people are **really** saying is a big step toward alleviating your ignorance.

10. Government IS taxes, of course; and another wise man has noted that the power to tax is the power to destroy. Government is a parasite that invariably eventually destroys its host, even though the government always dies along with the society it has cannibalized.

11. So far the parasite has always sprung up again, but there is some hope. You are reading this book. And you make all the difference.

12. To the people that make their living from their self-proclaimed monopoly over the definition and dispensation of justice, you are only so much meat to go through the grinder.

13. You are not in their sphere to attain justice, you are there to provide them with an income: some find it a very rewarding pursuit, but even the janitor can

feel superior to the miserable wretches huddling despondently along the courthouse walls.

14. Most of the patrons of the justice industry participate unwillingly, to the extent that the industry is often symbolized by its uniformed representatives. This eager sales force even arms itself and sallies out to capture customers off the streets.

15. And still the industry runs in the red every year, and needs taxpayer subsidies to keep it afloat.

16. The other face of an oppressive agency is best exemplified by advertising. Though they manipulate your emotions in every conceivable way, they have not yet found a way to get away with using force to persuade you to purchase their products.

17. But when their best success is based on convincing you that there is a fundamental wrong in you, and that only the use of their product can right that wrong, then you must recognize their probable motive.

18. Do not assume automatically that they mean you harm. It is simply that your well-being has absolutely no bearing.

19. Such people, when motivated only by profit, are terribly dangerous. Be vigilant in resisting their blandishments.

20. Instead of insecurity, the education industry fosters ignorance. Obviously, the less you know, the more

powerful will be those who control the dissemina-
tion of knowledge.

21. Control over the knowledge of the workings of the
    human body, and especially over the pills and potions
    that ease the pain, keeps the medical monopoly intact.
    (At your expense, of course.)

22. Do not, however, tell your physician that he or she is
    nothing but a licensed pill pusher, or a witch doctor
    in a white coat. They will resent it, mostly because it
    is true. The ignorance and helplessness of their vic-
    tims guarantee the prosperousness of their empire.

23. Until recently, of course, the powers usurped by the
    medicine and religion industries were usually con-
    centrated in a single individual, or small group, who
    performed the duties of both. Then the priest class
    split into two distinct factions with a growing dif-
    ferentiation between their functions.

24. Of the two, it is safer to trust the medicine men over
    the ministers, as the greed and venality of the for-
    mer are more open.

25. The path of humanity back to the gods has not yet
    been mapped by any known religion. Many people
    have had a glimpse, and have tried to share it. Many
    have become enriched by so doing. Many have died.

26. Religious leaders love to deck themselves in gems
    and precious vestments, purchased always by the
    contributions of their subjects. The enrichment and
    empowerment of churchmen are procured by
    means as devious as they are destructive.

27. It is easy to capitalize on the desperate desire of every human to achieve the completion of finding themselves in the gods.

28. Loss of connection to the gods has helped teach humanity to feel fear. Loss of the ability to connect with other humans has helped foster the capacity for guilt.

29. Religions want you to feel fear and guilt so that you will submit to control. If you make yourself suitably unhappy now, they promise you will be happy later. In fact they will promise you anything as long as you will turn over your money.

30. Trust no one who threatens you with the wrath of their gods as the punishment for disobeying their orders.

31. There are no gods in religion.

# ∼Chapter 2∼

1. Neither the preachings of self-appointed moralists nor the tactics of professional bullies have ever served as more than a sop to the necessity of controlling man's essentially violent nature. Nor will they.

2. Such control can only, and must always, come from within the individual.

3. Self control is the product of self respect. Respect of self starts with understanding and acceptance of the self.

4. Unblinking recognition of the true makeup of humanity is absolutely essential to understanding how the formative events in human history surround and permeate every thread in the fabric of human society.

5. Knowledge of what mankind really is, and why, must begin with an in-depth understanding of how human life began.

6. The first impetus came after a climactic change so horrific and devastating it is mind-boggling in scope. Many, many species simply died out; many

more became so specialized that survival was purchased at the price of becoming an evolutionary dead end.

7.  But the ancestors of humanity found another escape. They turned into a new species, capable of adapting.

8.  Becoming a whole new species required the concurrent development of new systems of communication, social order, and sexual behavior.

9.  Of course the process has just begun, and the slapdash manner of the doing has been evident in the results.

10. The emerging species had great potential, but the greatest test was yet to come. The ability to adapt to massive and incredibly rapid changes became more and more a desirable breeding characteristic as the changes multiplied.

11. Foremost and most formative among these changes was that minor migration of the female genitalia. Basically, womankind invented the headache; and thus began the whole sad tale of the ecstasy, and the agony.

12. The adaptation of the female anatomy to its new environment went to the extreme, as such evolutionary developments are wont to do. But making females safe from the environment went too far when her reproductive access grew difficult for the male to reach.

13. The newly emergent race began to die out.

14. The movement of the vaginal access from the customary rear-entry placement to its present position took hundreds of generations, while copulation became increasingly difficult. Male frustration and female guilt became universal.

15. Finally one male with the right combination of inventiveness and aggressiveness observed the direction the mechanics of the situation were pointing, and decided to approach it from a whole new angle.

16. The woman did not see it his way; and his frustration at her unreasonableness was compounded by his increasingly thwarted lust. When persuasion did not work, he finally was driven to coercion.

17. Then he slunk away from her sobs, leaving her not from callousness but from confusion and helplessness. Swamped with guilt and despair and consequent anger, he resolved never to touch her again.

18. Then he saw her again.

19. When his anger subsided, and his lust mounted, he begged her for forgiveness. Thinking he had regained his sanity, she gave it.

20. And he, believing she understood the new order, did the same thing again.

21. No one had a choice, and no one is to blame. The drive of life for life does not require men and women to get along, only to copulate. It was a desperate solution to a desperate situation, and it still functions in essentially the same way.

22. The forms that men and societies have devised to control and channel the tremendous force of that drive for life—namely seduction, marriage, and prostitution—have been wildly successful when compared with man's attempts to control the other half of his nature.

23. It is not correct to say that sex and violence are important in the structure of man's society.

24. Sex and violence **are** the structure of man's society.

# ~Chapter 3~

1. Women do not reject the advances of most men out of perversity, any more than the faithlessness of men is an indication that men are basically evil.

2. The real dark age for humanity was at its inception, when hundreds of generations came into existence as the result of forcible sex. The solution was gradually improved upon in several ways over the succeeding millennia.

3. One of the compensations was developing a sex drive which cannot begin to be matched by any other species.

4. Another was courtship rituals, which served a dual function. The ritual allows a man to approach a woman in a 'civilized' fashion, but more importantly it allows the woman to be selective.

5. One of the main misunderstandings between men and women stems from the fact that they have different genetic needs. The man is driven to spread his seed far and wide, to maximize genetic varia-

tion; while the woman's goal is to select for the best possible babies.

6. From the standpoint of the gene pool these complementary drives are elegantly functional, but they play hell with the psyche of every human being over the age of five.

7. Thus we have the woman: assaulted and abandoned, too exhausted to fight anymore; she grew permanently confused, afraid and ashamed. Always hoping he will be nice again, like he used to be, is as old as woman herself. So is being disappointed.

8. Modern man, however, was born of the pain of rejection. He did not understand why she was making it so hard for him (even though it was not **her** decision—he's not quite into logic yet, he just feels), and even less did he see why she got so upset when all he did was what he had to do. Besides, she asked for it.

9. Thus he is hurt, and embarrassed, and unsure of himself. He wants as little to do with women as possible, and simmers at the unfairness: after all, she was the one who made it difficult in the first place.

10. That Homo Sapiens has re-learned the art of reproduction is evidenced by the rate at which they are filling their planet.

11. What now needs to be known is what damage was done in the process, to the hearts and minds and souls of human beings, and how to begin to counteract that damage.

# ∼Chapter 4∼

1.  The first reason self esteem is so difficult to attain is mankind's terrible heritage.

2.  The second reason is the enormous number of people who can find some profit in your built-in feelings of inadequacy.

3.  The less a person is able to control themself, the more desperately they will attempt to control the lives of others.

4.  The harder a person struggles to exert power over the actions of others, the harder it is for that person to acquire or retain even an imitation of self respect.

5.  Such a person must constantly fight to ignore the voice of the gods within: the voices that would tell them that not only is what they are doing dreadfully wrong, it is pitifully futile. You can NEVER learn self control by trying to control another.

6.  The only difference between the architect of the "Final Solution" and the bureaucrat who finds a reason you can't have what you need, is a difference of degree, not of intent.

7.  The ability to do senseless violence is an inherited trait. The desire to control other people is not, and the undesirability of such an attitude is easily demonstrated. Simply observe the unfortunates who pursue this filthy practice most assiduously; and you will see at once that they are invariably the most self-righteous and unhappy people on Earth.

8.  The worst and worst off, of course, are those that pretend that their sole motivation is the good of their victim. You wouldn't try so hard to save someone else's soul if you thought **you** had one.

9.  Control over the lives of others is usually materially as well as emotionally rewarding. The oppressive agencies find it laughably easy to tap into the fear and guilt that people are already struggling with.

10. Once people are convinced that their failures are their own fault and look to an outside agency to save them from themselves, it is simple to convince people to shell out money to any charlatan who offers plausible-sounding protection.

11. A bully who decides he wants to be king will offer to refrain from doing violence to you, and to keep others from doing such violence. All you need to do is follow his orders and give him your money.

12. A smaller invader of a different sort will require you to subject yourself to someone with a similar monomania. Disease or injury mean seeking out a medicine man, with the attending injury to both

dignity and pocketbook, and leaving scars worse than the original wound.

13. Religions that threaten awful consequences to any person who does not obey and pay also tap into that basic fear and guilt to exist. The condition of your soul is not really their concern.

14. The gods do not wish to be worshipped, do not need to be propitiated, and really **do not** respond (except with humor) to bribery. Before you make a deal with anyone about the hereafter, talk to one of their satisfied customers.

15. The sexual and emotional guilt that humanity labors under makes reproduction a fertile area for interference by religion, and it is child's play to tap into a universal body insecurity in order to sell useless and harmful products.

16. Selling a product by extolling its virtues is entirely appropriate, even if the actual advertisement goes beyond all bounds of good sense or bad taste.

17. If you are afraid you smell bad, bathe.

18. But persuading a person to buy your product on the basis of a fundamental wrong in that person, which only your product can cure, is a nauseating manipulation of your fellow man. And very few people suspect just how damaging are the aftereffects of such a campaign.

19. The scars inflicted by the justice industry, however, often represent a trauma from which the person involved will never recover.

20. The main reason this pernicious blight thrives on society is that everyone already feels guilty; but being able to threaten people with a fate worse than death is a great convincer too, especially as people are predisposed to be frightened in any event.

21. Fear is a survival mechanism bred in over eons. Guilt is pro-survival because it keeps men from clobbering to death too many breedable females in their attempt to perpetuate the species, and because women keep taking them back after anything less.

22. You are built to experience fear and anger and guilt at the drop of a hat. You don't have a chance in hell of controlling those feelings as long as there is so much to gain from exacerbating them: there will be someone to profit from your pain any chance you give them.

23. If mankind is the product of Original Sin, the sin is that of the gods and not of man; and if there is forgiveness involved, you should be offering it instead of asking for it.

24. Please stop asking for it.

# Formative Testament:
# If This Were the Real World

## Book Four

# Fair is a Four Letter Word

# ∽Chapter 1∽

1. The second American revolution was the most successful coup d'etat in history.

2. It was not only almost bloodless, it damn near went completely unnoticed.

3. The first revolution was six years of blood and thunder and bought six years of freedom and peace. But the gentle anarchy of that sweet period was far too tempting a prize to those who hungered to control. They moved into a power vacuum and took over.

4. A handful of greedy men drew lines on maps and appointed themselves 'representatives' of these arbitrarily shared out areas. They met in secret conclave: using a remote local incident as a pretext, and securing the cooperation of a popular general, they announced their takeover.

5. There were some very questionable court decisions in the very courts they had created (and a couple of strategic assassinations) needed to secure their positions, but before anyone could catch on and

stop them, they had control of the machinery. (Read that, "of the guns".)

6.    Men fought the first American revolution so they could be left alone. The second revolution assured no one would be.

7.    Those who strove to preserve liberty in the second revolution fought most valiantly; and though they lost, the impediments they managed to put in the path of the power grabbers stood firm for over a century.

8.    **Control a being's economy and you control the being.**

9.    Governments usually have two main methods for control of the beings within their sphere. Monopoly of the money supply, and taxes, are their favorite weapons against you.

10.   By making itself the sole arbiter of the value of money, the government controls what you can receive in exchange for the hours of your life. If the money loses value, correspondingly does your life lose value. You allow the government to decide what your life is worth.

11.   If your money is worth nothing but a politician's promise, so is your life.

12.   You are not allowed to substitute any other symbol that has value to you, such as sea shells or silver coins: making one particular form of money 'legal

tender' makes it by definition illegal to tender any other kind of money.

13. It would take real talent not to enrich yourself when given only those conditions (power to determine the value of the money and power to put people in jail for using any other kind of money); and when you also have carte blanche to extort any amount you please from anyone who does earn some money, the people you are 'governing' are certain to be almost as hopeless as they are helpless.

14. This wholesale extortion is mostly done, oddly enough, to pay for people's rights. There is a great confusion in the world about rights. A 'right' means you are entitled to restrain others from doing something to you.

15. If on the other hand you are out of touch enough to assert that you have a "right to…" (food, shelter, medicine, etc.), you are actually proclaiming the right to force another to provide those 'rights' to you free of charge.

16. Producing **anything** of value takes work and sweat and worry and usually an investment. Having done these things gives the producers a right: they have the right to exchange their effort in the free market for whatever they can get.

17. They also have a right to refuse to support professional victims. If your only claim on their efforts is your need, why should they provide?

*18.* A need is not a right. Ever.
     Let's try that again, shall we? Say it with us…
      *18.* **A Need Is Not A Right.** (See? We knew you could get it. One day very soon, you all will.)

*19.* Need can never confer the right to force another to provide.

*20.* There is only one possible explanation for a society allowing its rulers to extort the massive sums needed to support the large bred underclass that the rulers keep as pets. Since members of this class do not in fact usually vote, any rationalization based thereon is void. But there is a reason.

*21.* Every human being comes with a vast reservoir of guilt, anger, and fear. The manipulators have had millennia to learn how to tap into these plush pools of emotion that make people so human. And they make good use of the knowledge.

# ~Chapter 2~

1. It is as foolish to dismiss slavery as a useful social function as it is to base that condition on religion or gender or race.

2. Those who wish to be slaves should be allowed to do so. Those who do not wish to should not so do. But those who do not wish to, have the right only to choose for themself. Simply because you do not wish to do a thing, you do not acquire the right to keep others from doing it.

3. Should a society decide to accept reality (well, it **could** happen) and take notice that a great many people do not **want** to take care of themselves, the creation of an acceptable alternative would appear miraculous as multiple problems in society moved simultaneously toward solutions.

4. Indentured servitude was an honorable tradition in the early days of the United States, but the system broke down when they started simply keeping their workers.

5.  Most people in that country believe their Civil War was fought to free the slaves, but nothing could be further from the truth.

6.  It was fought because the gene pool of the instigators had grown stale.

7.  Too small a percentage of the population was moving into and out of the area. Too many people were spending their entire lives in one place, and **way** too many people were marrying their cousins.

8.  The human being is a semi-nomadic animal.

9.  Small roving bands with maximum exogamic opportunity promote the happiest, healthiest individuals. Settling down is the first step on the road to stagnation and decay. Any artificial impediment to people's free movement greatly hastens that process.

10. Repeated inbreeding within a limited gene pool will produce a stable new line if the culls are kept from breeding back into the main line. This will have a tendency to cement desirable characteristics.

11. Repeated inbreeding within a limited gene pool **without any culling** brings disaster to the pool every time.

12. The situation was exacerbated in the American south by the presence of two distinct and largely separate gene pools. The smaller group was shuffled around to maintain exogamic health, but the larger group paid a devastating price for their unsound breeding practices.

13. Inside an already drastically limited gene pool, these people made it a point of pride to marry within their own circle, and their children and grandchildren did the same; and as the basic human drive for genetic variety created pressure, it again awakened the human capacity for slaughter.

14. The desperation of such a situation can be gauged in hindsight by measuring the devastation left behind.

15. The ratio is roughly one to one: for each person killed, there will be one person displaced. You can tell after a conflict how much exogamic relief was needed by counting the refugees and the dead.

16. Mankind will stop having wars when he learns to spot such trouble spots before the situation requires bloody alleviation, and begins to take other measures.

17. The American civil war was not fought over King Cotton or State's Rights or slavery. It was fought because the gene pool erupted.

# ᕄ Chapter 3 ᕄ

1.  Very few slaves were captured and taken to the Americas in chains. Many were purchased in Africa and along the Mediterranean; many more were bred in the United States. By the Civil War every slave was descended from at least six generations of slaves, and many from a dozen or more.

2.  Unsound as were their breeding practices among themselves, slaveowners often showed more sense when causing their horses, dogs and slaves to propagate.

3.  Unfortunately for the descendants of those slaves, the characteristics a smart slaveowner will breed for are the antithesis of the qualities needed to survive in a very competitive society.

4.  "The cowards never started, and the weaklings died on the way."

5.  The United States is an anomaly, containing as it does inhabitants from every other gene pool on Earth.

6.  And every single immigrant group displayed three survival characteristics: the courage to decide to go,

the initiative to get there, and the strength to survive the journey.

7. They were self-selected from within their home gene pools as the best and the bravest, by opting for a totally new environment. (Recall the ancestor of humanity that opted for becoming aquatic over dying out.) Those that made it to America represented the best humanity had to offer.

8. They then underwent a second culling, just as drastic, when they arrived.

9. The hardy survivors have bequeathed to their descendants the most competitive and capable society on Earth.

10. Casting newly freed slaves loose to fend for themselves in that frothing ocean was throwing so much meat to the lions. The poor bastards never had a chance.

11. It is incomprehensible cruelty to breed a people for generations toward docility and acceptance, and then dump them like so much garbage into the most cutthroat and competitive society man has ever devised.

12. Most of them sank immediately to the bottom of that society, of course; and this is why most of their descendants there remain.

13. Passing laws to make such people 'equal' is as effective as decreeing Pi equal to three.

14. Those who decide to appoint themselves representatives of a particular racial group, and demand for

that group special privileges and subsidies, are apparently acting from the premise that the racial group can not produce individuals capable of competing freely in an open market.

15. It is economically unsound to refuse to hire the best candidates for a job: it pays to disregard whether that candidate spends his time praying to the East, wears his skin in a different color, or comes to work in a wheelchair. Such foolishness brings its own punishment in the loss of profits.

16. Obviously it is economically unsound to require an employer to hire a less qualified candidate, especially as the politically favored minorities achieve that status by claiming lack of ability to compete.

17. Less obvious are the corrosive effects on the society, of using force to make others pretend that a socially handicapped person is 'equal' to those who do the actual work.

18. The ruling class is entitled to keep all the pets they want, but not by forcing others to care for them.

19. Foisting one or two pampered favorites onto an unsuspecting workplace is a silly and pointless attempt to make those unfortunates appear something other than what they are, and it fools no one. Shoving them in alongside real wage earners is a tragedy and a travesty.

20. It is a travesty to force others to give lip service to someone's supposed equality, while that someone

demands special privileges and subsidies for lack of the same.

21. It is a tragedy, for a government whose very existence is questionable, to force millions of productive people to spend half their lives working to support a bunch of strangers. Strangers who never have and never will give anything back.

## Book Five

# Therefore Choose Life

# ~Chapter 1~

1.  Refraining from masturbation causes people to become liars.

2.  Contrary to popular belief, American society does not emphasize sex and violence; in fact people seem to spend extraordinary amounts of energy trying, with varying degrees of success, to suppress these things. And with good reason.

3.  People simply do not understand the sheer magnitude of the human sexual drive. The twin drives of any organism are to survive and to reproduce. If survival is no longer such a challenge for much of the Earth, that leaves lots of energy for....

4.  Even as poorly as men and women communicate today, it is a near impossibility to imagine that time when the sex act simply stopped working for people.

5.  One side effect that is easy to see nowadays is what happened to the male of the species. All this has taken place in such a short period, the male has had no time at all to grow accustomed to the fact that his target has moved.

6.  Many men fixate on where it used to be, and accept another male as a sex object; for another male at least has a bodily access in roughly the right area.

7.  But the classic male 'vagueness of aim' can result in a man fixating on something widely removed from reproduction; such as needing certain clothing or props for his satisfaction, or forming an inappropriate bond with another species that has a target in approximately the right place.

8.  Female homosexuality springs from the same sexual crisis, and serves as a reminder that the race would have died out from the violence were it not for the forgiveness of women. Some women simply reject the violence with their souls, and cannot accept men.

9.  Homosexuality does not concern the majority because it is genetically self-correcting. Being unable to father children can never, by definition, be passed on to the next generation.

10.  But in each crop of babies is a small percentage that are going to be overwhelmed by all the fear and guilt and confusion that now define sex. They are self-selected losers in the only game in town: you may feel sorry for them if you wish, but they are no threat to your world.

11.  The sexual problems of individual humans are **totally unimportant** to the gene pool. As long as a sufficient number of men can propagate, the rest can go kill each other or sleep with each other or set up monastic societies. The human race has been

through some very rough times, and those who accept love where they find it are just being human.

12. And human is so hard to be!

13. Much of the pain in every life is not your fault, but is the result of two circumstances. With knowledge you can overcome one and shield yourself from the other.

14. The first cause of human troubles was that dual betrayal, first by the world, and then by the opposite sex.

15. They were betrayed by an environment that had shaped and nurtured them for millions and millions of years. There is a residue in every human today of a vague feeling of being cheated, and this is one of the causes.

16. Mankind has never quite trusted his world since, and this can account for the tremendous energy with which he strives to control the physical world.

17. The second great cause of both humanity and human misery is the host of difficulties brought on by the failure of sex. They had every reason to expect a system perfected over those same millions of years to go right on working.

18. But it **stopped working.**

19. If you awoke paralyzed, or came home to find your house missing, you would come nowhere near the feelings of anger and loss and disorientation that the whole human race was simultaneously experiencing.

*20.* The universal feelings of betrayal and lack of trust, of fear and guilt and anger, and the tremendous human load of confusion and despair, all cause each person to have the same sad feeling: self-doubt.

*21.* This can be the most destructive of emotions. When everything you have ever counted on becomes untrustworthy, you can't help wonder if you might be doing something wrong.

*22.* Some self-questioning is natural and healthy and useful. Too much doubt can paralyze and make you doubt: your perceptions, evaluations, and even your own experience.

*23.* This is the core of human misery. That built-in, inescapable well of self-doubt leaves you a breeding ground for the fear and anger and guilt, and the confusion and despair, and the pain. These feelings are a life sentence for every human born.

*24.* The good news is that parole, with good behavior, is distinctly possible.

# ∼Chapter 2∼

1.  No one profits from your happiness. Except you, of course.

2.  A great many people derive financial or emotional benefit from your unhappiness. It is difficult and unprofitable to try to manipulate people that are strong and free. It is always to a ruler's advantage to find your every possible weakness and exploit it.

3.  If you are hungry, they will promise to feed you. They like for you to be frightened so you will feel a need for protection. And above all they foster your confusion; for when you come to them with questions, they get to define the answers.

4.  Up until now, you have not been responsible for the state of the world, for no being can be held liable for actions taken as a result of misinformation.

5.  And boy, have you been mis-informed!

6.  You have had no choice but to accept what you are told by those who claim suzerainty over your soul, if they have been your only source of information.

But from now on, you must choose: to remain ignorant and fear-ridden, or to be free.

7.   There is a difference between an inherited behavior
     and that which is universally learned. Fear and
     hatred of the unknown are **not** natural reactions.

8.   They may be very common reactions, but they do
     not have to be automatic. Humanity has had to
     learn hate.

9.   Suffering from a vast and easy-to-reach reservoir of
     self-doubt, the average person is a total pushover
     for the manipulators. And though fear and confu-
     sion and self-doubt make it easy to rule a man,
     those handy handles on your soul are not a patch on
     how simple it is to twist a man's mind once he
     learns to hate himself.

10.  And that is their real secret.

11.  If you can be taught to hate yourself, you will not only
     believe anything you are told and do anything you are
     told to do, you will be pathetically grateful to your
     life's destroyers as long as they seem to have answers.

12.  The question of whether a human life has absolute
     value is now debated with the same ferocity that
     used to be granted to the number of angels on the
     head of a pin. The answer is no, it does not: your life
     has value only if it has value to you.

13.  Always question the agenda of a person who tries
     to make you admit that every life has value. What
     they really want is validation; for if you think every

life has value, then by definition they have forced you to concede that **their** life has value.

14. Even more dangerous are those who shrill for equality. There is no such thing this side of the grave. There are many in whom confusion and self-hatred have turned into a hatred of all life. Beware of anyone who demands everyone be equal; they are really calling for universal death.

15. Warning: it is not politically correct to value your own life above, or even as much as, that of others.

16. It is impossible to overstate the negative effects that the strenuous formative events have had on the human psyche. There would be no human race had those events not happened. All that remains now is to clean up the debris.

17. First you must believe that there are people on Earth that have suffered from humanity's heritage. And that fear and guilt and self-doubt can turn into hatred; first of one's self, then of anyone who does not appear to suffer as much.

18. There are many who give lip service to good works while secretly hating all humanity. The propaganda of the oppressive agencies have convinced these pathetic specimens that they are completely worthless.

19. Pathetic? Yes, because society teaches you that you are right not to trust yourself or others; that you have surely done something wrong, and they are going to get you; that nothing you do is right but

you had better keep doing it; that you deserve to be miserable, but it is your fault if you are not happy.

20. They teach you to hate your life, but that you may not end it.

# ~Chapter 3~

1.  It is not socially acceptable to end your own life, but there are no eyebrows raised when a person chooses to have society take their life.

2.  Multiple murders is a pretty sure ticket, especially if rape and torture are involved. Killing a police officer is good, for instance, as is assassination of a politician.

3.  It is time to end that suffering of innocents caused by those who wish to die.

4.  Suicide is a sin in most religions and a crime in most locales, and for good reason. Those who cry out with the most hysteria against suicide are doing so because they are afraid of it. Knowing as they do the worthlessness of their own lives, they are terrified that making suicide an acceptable choice will make it obvious that they should choose it for themselves.

5.  Blame them not, for they are the logical end product of all those expert manipulations. Having achieved a politically correct state of mind, they find themselves desperately unhappy. There is little

hope for those in whom the process has progressed so far.

6. You can not hate them for their sorrow—they can do a far better job of it than you can anyway—but you must resist, every moment of your life, their attempts to make you feel as they do.

7. "Peer pressure" is the use of social ostracism to force another to behave or dress or speak as you do; and it is the first manifestation of self-doubt. The more people you can force to behave just like you, the easier it is to tell yourself that you are indeed doing right.

8. A secure man will neither strive to be different nor try to make others be as he is.

9. You know you are right by listening to the gods within you. No amount of social approval can justify doing that which you know to be wrong.

10. Humanity is not a finished product. Having neither a blueprint nor even an artist's conception to go by, we are learning as we go. It has been a wonderful experiment, but it has backfired dreadfully; and unfortunately it is now up to you, the human race, to pick up the pieces and make this thing work.

11. Fear and guilt and anger were not mistakes, but they have become unnecessary baggage. They are no longer useful, but short of flipping the world over on its side again, there is no universal solution. Each human must learn to conquer his own pain.

12. When you have enough knowledge you can understand and forgive yourself. This is the second step.

13. It is easy to resolve that you will cease to be unhappy. But you have spent your whole life learning that you should be so, and it will require much practice to learn new mental habits.

14. The gods do not want you to be afraid. The gods do not want you to be ashamed. The gods do not want you to be painfully angry. The gods do not want you to be confused. The gods do not want you to be lonely. The gods do not want you to be sexually frustrated. The gods do not want you to doubt your own worth. The gods do not want you to hate your own life.

15. For further information, see Book Five, Chapter 3, verse 14.

# ~Chapter 4~

1.  People who hate themselves want you to hate your-self, too.

2.  If you acquiesce, you will prove that they are right to hate themselves.

3.  They do not **want** to hate themselves. It is simply that they have been overwhelmed by the fear, and the guilt, and confusion; and anger and finally despair. They have simply given up. They have stopped trying to be really human.

4.  You know the type—bitter, malicious, quick to find something to dislike in everyone—those that live on a perpetual diet of sour grapes, always making everyone around them feel uncomfortable and embarrassed. They never seem to have good expe-riences or happy memories.

5.  When your mother warned you that making a nasty face would cause it to freeze like that, she was telling you the absolute truth.

6.  Trust your instincts! Those little lines around the mouth are a dead giveaway that this person is full of

hate. When you get that hopeless, trapped feeling, the one that tells you that you are asking for help from the wrong person; when you realize that the grim delight they don't even try to hide is about to be had at your expense; when you dimly sense that they really **would** like you to get down on your knees; if you have figured out this much, then you can guess that you are in trouble. Go with that feeling.

7. Start practicing freedom. You do not have any responsibility to satisfy a bottomless pit. Their emotional needs cannot ever be met in the manner they try to meet them, which is torturing the helpless.

8. A cattle-prod wielder in a South American jail is more honest than the clerk that remands you, because of an incorrectly filled-out form, back to the end of the line. Both take pleasure in inflicting pain, but the clerk is usually more self-righteous about it.

9. Ask for a different clerk to serve you; go to another store. **Do not,** unless you absolutely must, feed into their power addiction. You don't have to hurt them, but you need to avoid them.

10. The worst possible betrayal of yourself is to allow these people to make you feel as they do.

# ∼Chapter 5∼

1. You have been told that the first step toward healing is knowledge, and the second is understanding and forgiving yourself.

2. The third step is understanding and forgiving others.

3. You will go a long way toward comprehending others when you start understanding yourself. The basic human model comes with a lot of garbage, and society tells him that he deserves more. Forgiving others will happen almost automatically as you begin to forgive yourself.

4. The world has taught you from birth that there is something wrong with you. Not overtly, for you would be able to resist that. It is in fairy tales and jokes and the threats your mother used to control you. The lessons children learn in school are not those found between the covers of books. They are in movies and songs and most especially in advertising.

5. A commercial advertisement which extols the virtues of a product is worlds apart from one that tries to convince you that feeding denatured, highly

processed foods to your family is necessary for you to be a good person; or that your every possible bodily function is faulty and needs to be artificially altered.

6.  Your sex life is such a prime target because that is the easiest way to manipulate you.

7.  Churches lead the hit parade in creating unnecessary horror for humanity. For one thing, every one of them is a scam: not one of those pulpit pounders has even the remotest clue.

8.  For the record, then: By the time eternity rolls around, you will have rejoined us; and we'll all chalk this one up to experience. Hell is right there on Earth.

9.  By claiming to know the will of a god, a religious man (-ipulator) claims for himself the power of that god. He demands tribute and imposes prohibitions in the name of that god.

10. Sanctimony and self-righteousness are not goodness. The religious person will tell you that they are.

11. The gods do not hate sex. We do not hate the human body. Sex is not inherently sinful, but the unclothed human body is inherently beautiful. We **are** humanity, and we do not hate ourselves.

12. The human sexual urge was heightened to such a vast extent in order to save the species. Sex was made pleasurable to persuade people to do it as much as possible.

13. The unpleasant emotional aspects of sex are basically unavoidable, so you ought to at least enjoy it when you can.

14. Any minister of souls who tells you otherwise is lying: his is a false creed. People only give away that which is worthless, so when he tells you to give your life to his god, what is he really saying to you?

15. It is your nature to be easily scared, and you have the basic human distrust of the world around you. He tells you his god made the world this way; and you are grateful someone has an answer, however foolish. He tells you to fear his god, and this will make sense; as you were born to be afraid of something, no matter how silly.

16. He tells you that you should feel guilty. (Boy, talk about a bingo!)

17. He tells you that sex is wrong. Since obviously there **is** something very wrong with sex, you buy that one every time.

18. He tells you that the heights of humanity are reached on your knees. Tell him to piss off.

19. A man who can manipulate your innermost weaknesses, and does so in order to worsen them; and who then offers a purported panacea for the very ills he has helped to create: only this kind of man can ask you to pay for the privilege of being 'ministered' to in such a destructive manner.

20. And this is all for the good of your soul!

# ~Chapter 6~

1. The good of your body, however, is the provenance of your government. Gods help you all.

2. Many churches have a nasty habit of torturing, killing, or excommunicating anyone whose property someone wishes to seize, or whose body someone wishes to savor. Ah, but the government! The government means business.

3. If religion has a saving grace, it is when it is voluntary. Government never is, only which one.

4. "From each according to their ability, to each according to their need." If there is a single sentence that will lead to the destruction of humanity, you have just read it.

5. That is indeed how we would like your world to work. But not by force. But Not By Force. BUT NOT BY FORCE.

6. A perfect government is a voluntary one, wherein every contracting citizen agrees to fulfill certain responsibilities in exchange for the protection and services of being 'governed.'

7.  The worst kinds of governments are those that
    resemble religions. "The State" is a fictional entity,
    and it is preposterously evil to assert that the rights
    and needs of a living individual are secondary to
    that of a fictional character.

8.  An effective government will also resemble a church
    in attempting to exacerbate your fear and guilt in
    order to control you.

9.  If there is a need to expiate the faults you were born
    with, it can only be met by accepting yourself and
    loving others. It can never be satisfied by prostrat-
    ing yourself to the glory of a god, or by giving your
    life in service to the state.

10. You are also born with the capacity for love and
    courage and joy; but these are rarely profitable for
    others.

11. Every politician instinctively knows that isolating
    the gene pool under his control is vastly to his ben-
    efit. A degenerating gene pool makes people feel
    dull, stupid and trapped: they realize that some-
    thing is wrong. Such people are far easier to rule
    than those who are brave, proud and confident.

12. It is absolutely contra-survival (for humanity) to
    teach people to hate and fear strangers.

13. Every government on Earth encourages this atti-
    tude, for it has a two-fold benefit. One result is the
    stagnating and easily controlled population; and the
    other is providing a rationalization for the govern-
    ment's existence.

14. Humanity never knew there was a difference between "us" and "them" until the government said so.

15. By tapping into your capacity for fear, the government creates a need, which it is then needed to meet. As in: those strangers are bad people and want to hurt you, but if you give your money and your freedom and your sons to the government, we won't let the strangers take your sons, money, and freedom.

16. It is pro-survival for the species whenever an individual chooses a mate from another gene pool, as such people are frequently the best products of their home towns.

17. Not every government overtly pursues a policy of racial purity, but all do pursue it. Mixed-race couples are anathema to every society, and the children of such unions are universally hated. This is diametrically opposed to your natural human desire to greet new people with interest, excitement, and enjoyment.

18. Practicing racial or religious or ancestral exclusionism works for the rulers because it awakens and provides a focus for all those nasty little feelings you come equipped with. People will allow governments to impose the most draconian measures, for their own good, as long as the rulers promise to protect them from 'the enemy.'

19. If this bullshit were the only insanity governments inflict on people, or even the worst, it would still be among humanity's most dangerous perver-

sions. But oh, the government always gives you much, much more.

20. Government is taxes. Never, ever forget that.
Never.
Ever.

21. It is staggering to contemplate the innumerable ways your government finds to intrude upon your personal choices and your private life.

22. Laws against 'vice' are the stock in trade of rulers. You are already good at guilt; god/vernment uses that against you with a vengeance.

23. It is no coincidence that government always cherishes to its bosom its own best products. Those most capable of being taught fear and hatred are naturally drawn to positions that give them power over others, that they might have a chance for revenge on any who dare to enjoy life more than they. These people do indeed hold pleasure inherently sinful, and wish to keep everyone else from having that which they cannot have.

24. Manipulating your guilt by virtue of your vices is not only a major support of the religion industry, it is the main occupation of government.

25. Their oppression touches all the bases: you pay people to make laws about things that are your concern alone; you pay people to punish you horribly for doing things that are no one else's business but yours; you pay the government to wage war against you for your totally private actions.

26. You may demand freedom only when you are prepared to act responsibly. A mature and self disciplined adult will govern their own actions far better than any outside agency could.

27. The government wants your life to be as bad as possible, so you will be easier to control; then they tell you that seeking any escape from their control is wrong; and that you wish to escape not because they are bad, but because **you** are. Then they use the guilt they have created as proof that you will do wrong if not tightly controlled.

28. Every human being instinctively embraces the philosophy of KYFHO.

29. One proof of this is the huge numbers of people that have allowed their god, or their government, or both, to try to turn them into sexless, emotionless drones.

30. They do so because it buys them at least a semblance of peace. When the alternative can be anything from humiliation to death, even the incredible oppressions of the communist governments will be publicly embraced by many who simply wish to be left alone.

31. It is the ultimate invasion to presume a right to judge, let alone try to **alter**, the thoughts in another person's mind. The tragic absurdity of a man killing another because someone chooses to think their own thoughts, is matched by the extremities of emptiness and terror the killer has to experience:

even the gods, who already know, find it hard to
understand why this person must kill.

32. This killer is the logical end product of the art of
the manipulators, of all the lies of the god-folk and
the governors.

## Book Six

# Quantum In Me Fuit

# ∼Chapter 1∼

1.  The meek shall indeed inherit the Earth; a piece about six feet by three.

2.  The garbage they are pulling on you is outrageous and not to be borne. The more you know of all the ways they oppress, the better chance you have of becoming free of them.

3.  **The justice industry is fueled primarily by vice.**

4.  It is your absolute duty to yourself and your fellow man that each choice that you make be a reasonable one. Given proper education, you can always make the right choice.

5.  Responsible sex does not spread disease or undesired progeny, but responsibility goes far beyond that. Consent to a sex act can be invalidated legally by incapacity to understand the act. Being too young, mentally handicapped, or intoxicated, can all preclude the necessary understanding.

6.  But a person can also be temporarily unable, through some trauma or stress, to contemplate all the consequences of their consent.

7.  Responsible sex neither takes advantage nor leaves broken hearts behind.

8.  Personal responsibility will provide all the control your sex life will need. Certainly more than the justice industry needs to (or can!) provide.

9.  Until very recently, sex was the vice of choice for cops around the world, but lately they all seem to agree that drugs are more fun.

10. In the year *1919*, the Volstead Act became the law of the land in the United States, providing criminal penalties for the manufacture and/or consumption of grain alcohol. Drinking booze immediately became the thing to do, and overnight a whole new class of criminals was created.

11. Professional lawmen suddenly saw tired old careers come roaring back to life. A vacuum opened up and people eager to control others rushed in to fill it. "G-men" were suddenly "in."

12. The end of Prohibition was an unmitigated tragedy for the justice industry, with all that lovely power and glory vanishing even faster than it had appeared. Their answer was to find a substitute for alcohol.

13. Until that time it was possible to buy cannabis, coca or opium, in bulk or concentrate, with ease and safety. Their use caused far fewer public problems than alcohol ever has.

14. For reasons you are now aware of, many people will positively salivate at the thought of depriving some-

one else of some pleasure. By appealing to this, and to the white majority's fear of other racial groups, they went on a crash program composed of equal parts fiction, hysteria, and sanctimony.

15. These machinations found such fertile ground in the early years of the New Deal for precisely the same reason that the Deal itself met with such acceptance. It was because their world had crashed and burned around them, and they had not a clue why or how it had happened; and they were looking for someone to blame.

16. (The Stock Market crash and the Great Depression did, by the way, both have the same simple and identifiable genesis; and were, in fact, ultimately caused by one action of a single individual. But more on that later.)

17. In Germany the people were engaged in a similar quest for a scapegoat. Stunned and shocked by the devastation of their society brought on by a collapsed economy, they seized upon a local religious/racial minority as the cause of their woes, finally bringing about the most horrifying chapter yet written in the story of man.

18. In America, they focused public hatred on those who chose to use recreational drugs.

19. When planning a pogrom, always select the most innocent and harmless for victims. There is much less likelihood they will shoot back when you attack them. People who only wish to be left alone, going

about their business and minding their own business, are by far the easiest to terrorize.

20. The U. S. government has taken its guide, in choosing who will be the victims of unearned persecution, from the likes of Pol Pot and Hitler. **More than half of the people in American jails and prisons have done no harm to any person or any thing.**

21. The jobs of millions depend on the continuation of this situation; and the power and glory of a self-appointed few requires the number of innocent victims to continue increasing.

22. And the artificially high prices of 'illegal' drugs does indeed cause enough people who believe they are already criminals to engage in enough crime to provide a significant portion of the rest of the justice industry's sustenance. Thus the real reason the industry opposes with such vigor the idea of just minding their own fucking business. Their living comes from drugs just as much as any 'drug dealer.'

23. Legalizing recreational drugs would immediately eliminate three quarters of the industry's business.

24. At this time, Americans can only dream of having room in their courts and jails and prisons for those who have caused actual harm to property or persons, and of police officers that spend their time on real crimes.

25. Given the massive failure of the justice industry to achieve any of their stated goals, many people are choosing to arm and protect their own selves. The

problem with any attempt to be responsible for yourself is the lack of the necessary support services; most especially the general unavailability of training in firearm function and safety.

26. Every citizen has a duty to be an active part of the fabric of society. Part of that duty is to arm yourself and contribute always to the safety and security of your community.

# ~Chapter 2~

1. Lack of enough of the gods in a man will make him a soulless animal; too much will make him crazy.

2. Y'all better do something **now**! Before we have to! There are way **waaaay** too many people on Earth, and you are poised on the brink of an explosive expansion that stupefies the imagination.

3. We have run out of souls. There are not enough to go around anymore, and too many people are being born without enough of the gods in them. We are beginning to be spread too thin. There are more people now alive than the total of all the people who have ever lived throughout history.

4. Your planet will comfortably hold and support between one half and one billion; no more. See to it, at once. You certainly know how, for gods' sake! (Cut your birth rate, of course. Every child has the right to be desperately wanted.)

5. Always are the ones without a soul drawn especially to positions of power over others, and for them the justice industry is a lovely place indeed: the luckiest

among them are even awarded the exclusive right of going armed.

6.   The definition of gods in human culture is essentially 'those to whom are reserved special powers over humans, especially the power of life and death.' The "Oops Theory" is what makes cops in America secretly believe they are gods.

7.   The Oops Theory simply means a police officer has a license to kill whomever they like, as long as they afterward recite the ritual formula: "Oops, I thought I saw a gun!"

8.   It matters not if the object turns out to be a long-handled comb, a cellular phone, or a sodapop can. The officer has achieved his objective, bagged his prey.

9.   A much preferred refinement of the theory is to actually see a real gun; first in your glove compartment wrapped in plastic, next seen on or near the 'criminal,' perhaps even in the bad guy's hand. One may wonder how often an independent lab would find microscopic bits of baggie upon examining such a weapon.

10.  Citizens would mob the precincts were they to discover how frequently this sequence really occurs.

11.  Of course, being mobbed by honest citizens is the worst fear of any bully, armed or not; and police agencies usually react with barely controlled hysteria to the suggestion that citizens go armed.

12. A cop thinks he has achieved the position of a god, but it is a pretty shitty deal. He doesn't get the respect a god should get, and he certainly doesn't get the pay. Awesome as their power already is, they usually compensate for their 'raw deal' by abusing that power as much as they can get away with. His gun is the only thing that makes him special.

13. When a policeman asserts that he wishes to end crime, you should wonder why; for that would mean the end of his job. With no crime there would be no reason for him to exist; but he would not cease to exist, he would simply become unemployed. There is nothing more useless than an unemployed god; and if you really believe he desires only to turn himself into a living Edsel, we have some bridges for sale....

14. **An armed, trained, and resolute populace is mutually exclusive with violent crime.**

15. Anyone who wishes to end crime will embrace such a populace with their whole heart. How then can anyone explain the violence of the opposition with which any hint of this idea is always met by those who claim to want to protect society.

16. If this were the real world, the cop on the street would not differ much from the waiter or the truck driver. The waiter wants to sell more food, work more hours, make more tips, and maybe aim for headwaiter. The driver hopes more people produce more products to be shipped, so he can earn more.

17. And if there are real humans employed by any
    police agency, those humans also want raises, over-
    time, and promotions. They want their department
    to have more business and they want to benefit
    from the increase.

18. After *14* years of vigorous expansion, law enforce-
    ment everywhere was looking at the stark desert of
    budget cuts. In order to keep the glory years alive,
    they overlooked one minor detail: this time there
    was no constitutional mandate to prohibit private
    use of recreational drugs. The Volstead Act set the
    precedent; the Federal Government does not have
    the power to make any recreational drug illegal.

19. But in a move that strongly echoed the persecutions
    of Nazi Germany, they focused on the helpless
    minorities in their midst.

20. Of course there was no factual content to the claim
    that the private recreations of Blacks, Mexicans, or
    Chinese were in any way a threat to society. So fic-
    tion was supplied wherever exaggeration was insuf-
    ficient; and was skillfully combined with political
    pressure to greatly magnify a minor public reaction.
    The result was a still misunderstood mixture of
    pure-drug laws and import taxes, and this junk was
    enough to get the persecution ball rolling.

21. Colombian drug lords with millions in cocaine are
    liable to shoot back; otherwise a drug arrest is a per-
    fect crime. You have the crime, the evidence, and the
    criminal in one fell swoop; you don't have to do any

actual investigating; and your arrest/conviction ratio will reflect a perfect one-for-one.

22. This is why there is no room in your prisons for violent criminals.

23. Police agencies everywhere pursue 'illegal drugs' with such aggression, not from a desire to protect society, but from a desire to protect their paychecks.

24. The police want to protect their juicy monopoly, and they always reserve their real outrage for what they perceive as competition. **They do not want citizens to be armed.**

25. Laws permitting gun ownership aside, you will never find a policeman who can remain rational while they try to discuss the idea.

26. But picture the following scene: A man walks into a fast food restaurant with an automatic weapon and guns down twenty-two customers and employees, all strangers to him.

27. Now picture the same man walking into a public place where all of the adults and some of the older teenagers are licensed gun wearers. Anyone stupid enough to try such a stunt will go down before the first innocent child can die; and the cops won't even be needed. Just call the coroner and go on with your meal.

28. When the government does not interfere with personal decisions, and violent crime has a hard time happening, there will be little need for the justice

industry as it now exists. Those functions truly needed by society will be supplied by the free market.

29. But since you must never end life unnecessarily, please do not kill all your lawyers. At least not yet.

# ∼Chapter 3∼

1.  Those that will shrill most loudly against the concept of legal, voluntary, contractual slavery will be those who secretly envy the slaves.

2.  But anyone willing to examine the idea logically instead of emotionally will immediately see some of the benefits to society.

3.  The most obvious one is a reduction in crime. The newly released prisoner, who at once commits another crime in order to be reincarcerated, would have an alternative. Even with appropriate retirement and medical provisions, the sale of a criminal's contract to a business or homeowner would both save society the cost of incarceration; and it would keep innocent citizens from having to suffer for someone else's twisted needs.

4.  This option should be open to everyone. If you want to take some time off—spend the next year or five or ten, letting someone else make your decisions and provide for your needs—you should have that option, without hindrance or disapproval from society.

5.  With provisions for the education, religious freedom, and optional family life for slaves; and minimum requirements in place regarding food, housing, and restrictions on physical discipline, it would become quite a fad among young people, and should be well accepted by many leaving the military.

6.  Problems in society will be easier to solve if your solutions are based on what man really is, rather than on what he ought to be.

7.  Legal, contractual, voluntary slavery could also be a substitute for tax-supported welfare programs. A person who is in a coma is usually unable to do any kind of work to support themself; but most others can do something that is of some value to someone. The standard slavery contract can be easily altered to deal with any kind of physical limitation, and all but the laziest will find negotiated work preferable to choosing between prison and starvation.

8.  Not even the genuinely unable have a right to force any other to provide for their support. Those who find modern life too complex, and competing too difficult, will have a respectable and responsible alternative.

9.  Another simple cure for some very serious social ills would be effected by allowing suicide as an accepted and responsible solution.

10. In Japan, honorable hara-kiri leads the list of self-culling practices that those people have evolved over the centuries to limit the size of their popula-

tion. These practices have created—in spite of severe space limitations and a total dearth of most industrial resources—an astonishingly competitive and successful society. We are not, however, advocating leaving baby girls out on the tops of mountains. (Don't be silly.)

11. Suicide in most locales is both a sin and crime. The former asserts that you belong to the local god; the latter is proof that your life is considered government property.

12. For-profit suicide clinics, providing a clean, safe and painless exit, would offer a decent alternative to leaving bloody remains for loved ones to find. And they will offer a choice to those who now feel they need to slaughter innocents in order to force society to take their life for them.

13. And those left unemployed by the dismantling of the justice industry could be put to work administering the slavery programs and suicide clinics.

# ∼Chapter 4∼

1.  Responsible recreational drug use includes more than refraining from driving drunk or committing crimes to support your habit.

2.  It means educating yourself about the side effects of the chemical you wish to use; such as, you may want to buy cancer insurance if you wish to smoke cigarettes.

3.  If you claim the right to rule your own choices, you must always be ready to act responsibly. Pay your bills before you buy drugs, go to a movie, or put a fiver on a horse.

4.  Universally responsible sexual behavior will automatically eliminate welfare mothers and deadbeat dads. Simply put, you **must** be aware that you are risking a *20* year sentence each time you take off your clothes. No protection is perfect; if you can't risk it, don't!

5.  To gracefully relate to the opposite sex you need humor, patience, maturity and self acceptance.

Most people can't even spell those words when they become sexually active.

6. Self restraint is an intimately human accomplishment, but it is not to be seriously expected from the quivering bundle of confusion and raging hormones which puberty causes each human to be. They are unlikely to find either themselves or control thereof.

7. The sex act can sometimes bring transcendent joy. This joy requires fulfilled and educated individuals. Such individuals can develop from self knowledge, but the availability of such information is severely limited. Children need to learn to love and accept their bodies, not to hate and fear them.

8. People advocate against child sexual education for the same reason they support any other intrusion into your life: they are scared shitless that someone may enjoy themself.

9. This fear—that someone has something that you haven't—is so pervasive mainly because you are continuously being exhorted to nurture your negative emotions.

10. Human beings have almost no chance of developing a good relationship with the opposite sex; but teaching self knowledge and self acceptance to children will go a long way toward growing healthy adults. Since you who read these words have probably missed that chance, you will have to educate yourself.

*11.* The acceptance begins when you understand how you all got into this mess. You know about the drastic climactic and physical changes that have shaped the human race, and the dreadful scars that the shaping has left behind. We are not apologizing: you will get no welfare from the gods because your ancestors were mistreated.

*12.* You have what you have; so deal with what is, instead of what a "fair" world would have given you. It is all up to you now. You get no breaks for your handicap, for everyone labors under the same one. All you can do is make the best of what you have.

*13.* Accepting your faults can start a dangerous trend: you might start loving yourself. You are indeed here for a reason—count on it—we don't make **that** many mistakes.

*14.* Accepting and loving yourself will have a weird and wonderful side effect. The more you understand yourself, the more you will realize that everyone else hurts just as much as you. And the more you accept your feelings, the easier it is to see that other people may have even less chance to be happy than you have; and the easier it is to be gentle with them, and to be grateful for being you.

*15.* This will not turn you into a social worker or a Sunday school teacher: just the opposite. The traditional image of these grim, sexless, joyless people is not one of self love. It is an image that is usually associated, oddly enough, with those who have dedicated their lives to serving others.

16. There is no joy in selflessness. If there were, communism would work. But real joy **is** in true giving.

17. The high incidence of potency problems which plague today's man does not stem from his improper toilet training or lust for his mother. (Freud had some good insights but not enough knowledge.) Sure you are a mess. You have been taught to hate your body, your soul and your life. But you can change that now.

18. There are plenty of self-help books available: buy or borrow several, and take the best from each. There is no book, no magic of any kind, that will fix you overnight. It will take years of effort.

19. Keep in mind that you are trying to overcome not only the conditioning you have been warped by from birth; but you also have millions of generations behind you contributing to your despair.

20. You do have some tools on your side.

21. Unfortunately, those can **also** be used against you, and to your great detriment.

~Book Seven~

# "My God Can
# Beat Up Your God"

# ~Chapter 1~

1. There will never come a time when a politician will stand up and say, "Our gene pool is getting stagnant, therefore I am declaring war on our neighbor to the south."

2. Damned hard to raise an army with a slogan like that.

3. The genetic stability (and therefore the political, economic, and especially martial stability) of an area can be measured by consulting one of three primary indices. They are: the infant mortality rate, the percentages of new businesses that fail, and the number of people who live at least one day's travel from the place of their birth.

4. Low numbers, and especially falling numbers, on any of these indices are a clear danger signal. When all three are simultaneously and gradually dropping, it is time to shout "Warning! Warning!"

5. It means you are about to go to war.

6. A rising infant mortality rate is indicative of a healthy gene pool in two ways. First keep in mind

that a people who do not move are degenerating. But movement is risky, and the weakest always die.

7. Obviously, when the odds are against survival, those that live are the survivors. A moving populace is healthier because it is composed of a higher percentage of tested survivors.

8. The other reason a rising IMR points to genetic health is more subtle. Intermixture between separate gene pools is the best place to look for these favorable combinations. Many of the combinations work well; but many do not, and many of those that don't work as well will die at birth. Perhaps that is not how it 'should be,' but that is how it is.

9. The spirit of entrepreneurship is another face of the same reflection. More business failures means more people tried. Taking big risks is what got you here today; and as a survival quality, taking chances is essential both to societies and to individuals.

10. Of course the third measure of a stable culture, out-of-area-breeding, is just another way of saying the same thing. A gene pool on the move is a healthy gene pool.

11. The figure of one day's travel remains static regardless of the available local transportation. Exogamic relief comes when a sufficient proportion of the population engages in family making outside that limit. People who marry within their own gene group, and encourage their children to do the same,

are condemning their grandchildren to first stagnation, and then violence: there is **no** other alternative.

12. But we have left our poor politician standing there with nothing to say (gods forbid!)—he cannot possibly tell the truth, even were he to know it—and he needs to be utterly convincing when he sings the Cannon Fodder Song.

13. Come to think of it, your local draft board would not lack for recruits if they would only announce the real reason they need "a few good men."

14. Now there is a foreign exchange!

15. That will be the only long-term substitute for war, of course: large scale voluntary genetic relocation. You must encourage your young people to mate into another gene pool.

16. The measure of the sincerity of a do-gooder is the amount of his own cash he is willing to put up to finance his cause. Those who wish to end war can work toward their cause by paying for transportation and/or relocation bonuses. This will be much more effective, both in the short and in the long run, than such stunts as stopping traffic in the street.

17. No matter how desperate a politician may be to gain re-election or how greedy the makers of munitions may be, any attempt to stir up war fever will meet with all the excitement of a wet sparkler if the genetic pressure is not present. Likewise no Chamberlain can stop the tide of war once the spark has been ignited.

18. The pretext that serves to ignite the spark is usually considered the cause of the war. Whether the pretext is economic, religious, or to right a perceived historical wrong, war is indeed a magic charm for shoring up shaky regimes or for lining the pockets of warmongers.

19. But there is only one cause of war, and any other justifications are merely Cannon Fodder Song.

# ∼Chapter 2∼

1.  Evolution always happens one step at a time, and we are not working from a blueprint.

2.  We try to stop before any one development progresses too far (we don't want to have to do a "dinosaur" again!): keep in mind that most of the oddities you see at the zoo predate man.

3.  A species that grows too well adapted to its environment will perfect itself into an evolutionary dead end. The adaptability and variety of humanity, which can drive absolutely bananas those who live for rules, are among mankind's premium assets.

4.  Humans are simply the best we have been able to do so far. We have made mistakes with you, too: the worst one may turn out to be forcing you through too many changes too fast. If you do manage to kill each other off, that may be man's epitaph.

5.  On the other hand, it may yet be the making of you.

6.  You have passed another nexus: other than the action of an aberrant madman, you may not again

see your ultimate energy of life turned into cheap
and easy death.

7.  Unfortunately, this also appears to have made large
    scale war impossible. We are counting on you: you
    will find a substitute. Given that humans also seem
    to take such joy in physical destruction, it is likely
    that any alternative you stumble into will probably
    look a whole lot like war.

8.  Earth is the laboratory of the gods, and in a sense
    humans are the experimental animals; instead of a
    germ, you have been infected with a fever of the
    libido. **War Is An Expression Of The Human Sex
    Drive.**

9.  Another way of describing an evolutionary dead
    end is 'too much of a good thing.' That your explo-
    sive, overwhelming sex drive is so frequently turned
    to destruction is a regrettable excess, but you **must**
    concentrate on curing the disease: the symptoms
    will vanish of themselves.

10. (To be replaced by the side effects of the cure, no
    doubt. Ah, well. But we seek improvement, not
    perfection.)

11. To talk of a cure for war is laughable until you at
    least recognize the cause. Waiting until the numbers
    indicate that bloodshed is imminent will make pal-
    liative measures ineffective.

12. You must recognize that the need to move and mix
    is a critical part of the makeup of man. Thus it
    began with the beginning of man, and thus it will

always be. There is indeed a direction to our experiments, and the prime necessity is to constantly create new combinations, looking for winners.

13. The winners are not necessarily great scientists or artists or engineers. Simply going to work every day and raising a loving, gentle family can be a great thing to do with your life, as long as you cause no harm to others along the way.

14. The need to breed surpasses all others. Love and sex will continue to occupy every human mind; and it will be so, until far beyond a future you can see. Physical love is the embodiment of life's drive for life.

15. The direction you go from here is completely up to you.

16. Killing is never appropriate except in self defense. It is **never-never-never** the will of **any** of the gods that you slaughter each other, **especially** not on the pretext that it is being done to please one of us!

17. To kill in the name of a god is a crime against the gods, against humanity, and against yourself. It is never, ever pleasing to the gods when you hurt another "for their own good." Torture can neither bring a person to a god nor save anyone's soul.

18. Those who use force against another condemn themselves. Those who use force in the name of the gods may well be condemning humanity.

# ∾Chapter 3∾

1. The difference between a bomb-throwing hostage taker, and a self-righteous churchgoer who rails against the sins of others, is that the terrorist is more honest.

2. Learned men will tell you that people embrace religion in a search for justice, solace, and explanations. You will not find many who will tell you about the other big emotional payoff.

3. You get to feel bigger and badder than anybody else. You get to feel special. For many, that is the only way they **can** feel special.

4. You are not commanded to kill in the name of Krishna, Allah, Jesus or Jehovah. You are not even required to spread the word to the ignorant, though you are certainly welcome to enlighten all who request it.

5. There are indeed commandments, but you need not worry about breaking them. You cannot break the ones about which we really care. What you call such things as the laws of gravity and conservation of

energy are simply not on the same level as one of your self-imposed prohibitions.

6. Sin lies in hurting other people. Hurting yourself is not a sin, it is merely stupid. But causing other people needless pain is definitely a sin.

7. Hurting other people in the name of the gods is a scam to benefit first the priests, then the rulers, and always the priests. The things people can do to hurt each other may make us turn our heads, but the things done in the name of religion turn our stomachs.

8. To give them the benefit of the doubt, there may actually be the odd cleric who believes the garbage he tries so energetically to cram down your throat. There are surely some who try to believe, and they will try all the harder to convince you, so that they might drown out their own doubts. But most are outright frauds.

9. If you think you know something is would be of benefit to others to hear, then by all means, speak out. Write a book, teach a class; charge all the traffic will bear. Spread the word! But before you claim to speak for the gods, it would be best to check your facts. And you must tell the truth.

10. We do not object to anyone making a buck. But these charlatans usually have a god whose primary aspect is financial. We do not care for you inspiring your flock with fear and self-loathing and shame; then for a fee offering answers to the very doubts

you have created; and justifying this foolishness by blaming it on one of us.

11. If you are misinformed enough to believe that you have a mandate, or even permission, to pull this bull, you are hereby requested to cease immediately and return every cent of the extorted money.

12. If you are in the majority, and you consider your parishioners patsys or sheep, then we have nothing to say to you. Your victims will eventually say it, with sticks and bricks if not with bare hands. The day cannot come soon enough for us. Perhaps many more people will really have the chance to find the gods within, when these professional parasites are removed from the body of humanity.

13. It is never appropriate to manipulate negatively the emotions of another adult in order to influence their behavior, whether the profit be emotional or financial. Keep your fucking hands off.

14. We want you to be happy, joyous, and free; and anyone who tells you **anything** else is a liar. And anyone who lies to you in the name of the gods is a dishonest whore.

15. This repugnant bunch of slithering scum makes a profit from more than exacerbating your weaknesses and then blaming you for feeling that way. They also sell sanctimony.

16. The secret appeal for the churchgoer/terrorist is the right to put other people to death for enjoying life. The diffuse human potential for anger and the

feeling of being cheated can be stirred and simultaneously fed by a man with a plan. At a stroke they give you something to feel good about (I am pledged to my god and am therefore superior to all who are not), and they give you someone upon whom to look down.

17. Whether taking up the cross or the crescent, you can bet that the eager new convert is nursing secret visions of jihad and crusade. Those religions which best offer that opportunity attract the most 'devout' recruits.

18. The rapid changes you have been forced through have left mankind with a residue of feeling cheated. Being betrayed first by the world around them and then by their own bodies left behind a potential willingness to fall for the idea of a scapegoat. This is the secret of success for religions.

19. By assuring your disciples that the way they worship your god makes them better than those who do not worship so, you can assure yourself a faithful flock. But they will really love you when you proselytize your supposed god's command that they kill every other god's disciples.

20. You will never know enough about the gods that you may claim "one" is better than "other." You will never be commanded, requested, or even faintly desired to kill, based on such imaginary superiority.

21. We do not doubt that you will go on killing for some time to come. We do not underestimate the power of hate; nor should you.

## Book Eight

# It's Not Paranoia When They Really Are Out to Get You

# ~Chapter 1~

1. Humanettes are people who have not been rewarded for being good.

2. You are told that you must be "good" and that it will make you happy to do so. They define good as obeying god (or god's mouthpiece), the government, and the cop on the corner.

3. But the rules that oppressive agencies promulgate are not intended to make people happy. They are designed instead to turn people into sheep—witless morons who will hate and kill on command—and to keep the oppressors powerful and rich.

4. (At least it has not yet been suggested that people be killed for offensive body odor or bad breath.)

5. It is not in the best interest of any oppressive agency that you be allowed to be happy, let alone encouraged to be: and teaching you how to be happy is out of the question.

6. Take a being that has a natural capacity for pleasure and joy, but also carries a built-in tendency toward fear, anger, guilt, and self-doubt: then tell such a

creature that pleasure is a sin or a crime, and that they deserve to feel guilty and frightened. Tell this being that true joy lies in hating other races or religions or nationalities; that pleasure comes from suppressing natural instincts and desires so that they can more effectively obey your rules.

7. People who are taught that joy and pleasure come from hate and fear become rather confused, and this worsens their feelings of lack of trust and self-doubt.

8. This person will soon decide that no one is allowed to be happy; and that they must enforce whatever rules they can, and as vigorously as they are able.

9. Humanettes worship the rule. Whether it is "The Bible," the Army Manual, or a bureaucrat's regulations; if it is written somewhere that someone may not do something, there will be a stampede of Humanettes eager for the chance to forcefully apply that rule.

10. Even more sickening are the ones who assume for themselves the right to punish those who transgress against "The Rules."

11. The list of those to hate is endless, and consists entirely of those who in some way violate the 'rules' of the hater. You do not have the right to forcibly prevent acts or thoughts which you secretly wish you could enjoy.

12. For example, it is easy to hate a Drug User. You can never acknowledge that there is a need for anyone to find relief or escape from that which you are stu-

pid enough to tolerate. You are not afraid they will sell drugs to your kids: you are scared shitless that someone will enjoy themself.

13. The hysterical cries for the imposition of ever harsher penalties upon those who use recreational drugs are always cried by the self-righteous few, for they grow positively apoplectic if their own rules against pleasure are violated.

14. Humanettes are anti-life, and most do not even try to be human. They are people who can only derive pleasure from inflicting pain.

15. The social worker, who supposedly has given her life to better the lot of the unfortunate—and who incidentally resents and despises the people that make her life so "difficult"—can only cause pain by refusing to dispense the benefits she is there to dispense. And at night she dreams of using a cattle-prod to teach these people some respect.

16. And the churchgoer, singing about smashing evil-doers with such vindictive joy, would like nothing better than to smash a few himself.

17. The military is not classed as an oppressive agency for the simple reason that it is honest. Their job is oppression, and they make no bones about it. The Humanette may take positive glee from the authority a uniform gives, and the soldier may well enjoy raping and killing; but they rarely pretend it is for the good of the victim. ("We had to destroy the village in order to save it.") (Well, OK, they **rarely** pretend.)

*18.* Sanctimony and self-righteousness are corrosive
and soul sickening. It is more to the detriment of
those who feel it than to those of whom they disapprove. The moment you try to believe you are better
than anyone else, for any reason, you become an
emotional whore.

# ~Chapter 2~

1. Most prostitutes are bad businesspersons.

2. Far too many people are willing to sell their integrity dirt cheap. Allowing another to define the rules is to concede that you cannot make the right rules for yourself.

3. Churches and governments thrive by taking over your sex life. Causing you to repress your natural desires creates huge amounts of restive energy for them to channel as they will: appealing to people's worst instincts and providing a scapegoat for your unhappiness will get them hateful mobs every time.

4. Appropriate consent for a sexual act is obtained freely from one who is old enough to understand the consequences and emotionally stable enough to make the decision. As long as everyone present has given valid consent to whatever happens, you have our blessing.

5. Enjoying your own sexuality is easier when you start to free yourself from guilt. Recognize the source of the discomfort (man's amazing past), and

accept that you will always feel a bit like that. Then
ignore it and let the fun begin.

6. Approaching romance from a starting point that
consists of fear, lack of trust, guilt and self-doubt,
does not give most people a good start. Nearly
everything from Macho to mascara can be
explained as attempts to compensate for the basic
feeling, which everyone harbors, that you just don't
quite measure up.

7. That's all you need to know! Everyone else is just as
scared as you are. The more you can relax and enjoy
your potential partner, the less you will worry about
whatever impression **you** may make. Which makes
the best impression of all.

8. Then resign yourself to the inevitable. Men and
women have complementary traits, not identical.

9. Men are simultaneously afraid of rejection, and wary
of the clinging vine. Man's nature is always to spread
his seed as widely as possible; the average relationship lasts just long enough for him to believe a baby
has been started. Satisfied he has done his job, he
then moves on. It matters not if a baby has actually
begun: men and women are designed to lose interest
in each other after a period that will either deny or
establish fertility.

10. We neither approve nor disapprove of monogamy—
we find it interesting, if impractical—but man was
never designed for it, so please do not fault him for

lack of perfection in living up to a very unnatural standard.

11. A woman's inclination will always be to select the best possible father for her children, and she naturally prefers a different father for each of her children. Woman is no more designed for lifelong monogamy than is man.

12. The practice of monogamy is nearly universal now, and is mandated by most churches and governments. We believe there are two main reasons for this: monogamy means more control of private lives by outsiders, and it means less fun for everyone.

13. A unit of two seems too small to handle the complicated and difficult process humans have made of helping children survive to adulthood. A minimum of two men and two women would not only provide a taste of the needed genetic variety (for both sexes); it would also greatly ease the financial strain and the sheer emotional effort of coping with children, by spreading the care and expense among more adults.

14. A marriage contract should provide for two things: the division of mutually acquired assets, and continuing care of minor children. But an expanded marriage structure would make divorce nearly unnecessary.

15. More adults around to help meet your emotional needs would mean all the pressure is not on one person; and by the same token, you do not have to meet all the needs of another. And of course chil-

dren can **always** benefit from having more people around to love them.

16. And the infertility of a single partner in an expanded marriage may still be a heartbreak, but no longer a tragedy.

17. The above reasons are also why monogamy is so vigorously supported by oppressive agencies.

18. It is a fascinating puzzle that most legislators are men, and that most custom for prostitutes is men; but providing sexual services for profit is now always considered a sin and is nearly everywhere a crime. It is one thing for a lawmaker to feel that he himself should not patronize the professionals, but by no stretch of the imagination may he make that decision for any other.

19. And there is a special corner of purgatory reserved for the political parasite who passes a law concerning personal behavior; and then goes on doing the very thing he has forbidden to others, secure in the knowledge that his exalted position keeps him safe from prosecution.

20. It is a very crowded corner.

# ∼Chapter 3∼

1. The problem between men and women is the difference between men and women.

2. This appears to cause a great deal of profit to a great many people.

3. People that are already prone to massive self-doubt are easy to convince that the use of a particular toothpaste, cigarette, or automobile will make them attractive to the opposite sex. It also helps if you can persuade them that those who do not use your product will never be the object of anyone's desire.

4. People are bombarded from birth with a dual and very conflicting set of messages: that it is imperative that you make a connection with someone of the opposite sex, and that it is nearly impossible to so do. Add to this the preposterous notion that lust is bad (!), while a person is being entreated to buy every conceivable kind of junk on the basis that it will cause them to be objects of desire; and surprise! You will have some very confused and unhappy citizens.

5.  'When the going got tough, the tough got lusty.'
    The human sex drive was increased to such a
    degree that this organism could almost be said to
    possess only one of the twin drives; for in man
    alone does the desire to reproduce actually out-
    weigh the need for survival.

6.  If you are not already prone to think continually of
    sex, you are massaged with constant reminders that
    everyone around you thinks of little else.

7.  Once begun in a certain direction, evolutionary
    trends tend to keep going in the same direction as far
    as they can go. That the human sex drive was
    increased as much as it could possibly be, is evi-
    denced by the fact that it was still not enough; we had
    to take the final step.

8.  Obviously, the gods approve of lust! And it should
    be equally clear that a person who tells you other-
    wise is lying. We have already provided a brake on
    the process by limiting female fertility. You are
    now designed to find all sexual behaviors
    extremely pleasurable. These can include: thinking
    about sex, and reading or viewing of sexually ori-
    ented arts; holding, kissing, and touching another;
    and touching yourself.

9.  Imagine for a moment:
    You are born with a terrible fear of heights.
    Almost from that moment of birth, you are
    reminded continually that you will one day soon be
    required to leap from a tall cliff.

You are told many dreadful tales of how grue-
some is the fall, and how few survive it.

Heck, it's no wonder so many decide not to risk
the jump!

10. Fear both of sex and its repercussions is universal.
Many let that fear win: some enter monastic
orders or turn to their own gender, but many look
to the guiding lights in their society for answers.
(Poor bastards.)

11. Your sex drive is a wide-open socket for oppressive agencies to plug into, using your own energy
to compel you; to worship, to purchase, and to kill
on command.

Concatenative Testament:
# You Can't Have a Bible Without a Few Good Psongs

~Psongs, Book One~

# Your Children Are Not Your Children

# ∽Chapter 1∾

1. They are **ours**, and you will treat them as such.

2. There is a simple and lovely secret for keeping your sanity while attempting to control a child.

3. You are bigger than they are.

4. You can keep your sense of humor if you just keep that one fact in mind. You can compel them to do anything as long as you apply enough force; to the point that a parent can cause the ultimate lack of disobedience. (A dead child is never disobedient.)

5. But if your child is alive, you will find yourself constantly tempted to lose your temper. **Don't.** It can be critical, however, to simulate anger before you actually lose it; this can help you keep control of the situation.

6. Physical control of a child, especially at the beginning, is absolutely necessary for the security of a child. If you understand this and other needs of children, and strive to meet those needs and to set a good example, you will tend to turn out people who are brave, loving, and free.

7.  It is easy to convince a child that they are an object, and one of little value, before the mother's postpartum bleeding has stopped. Just handle the child mechanically when you tend to their bodily needs, and refrain from speaking to the child while you are doing the tending. You will quickly make an emotionless drone out of your little bundle of joy.

8.  But in case you have a hankering for offspring happy and healthy, you start first of all with example. If you are trying to love and understand yourself, your children also have a chance at self love.

9.  After birth, the first things your child will feel are being loved, which mostly means being held and fed (and whenever possible, breast is best); and pain, which is basically the lack of food or physical contact. Whenever holding your child, skin is best.

10. Skin is **always** best. If you soak a cloth in uric acid and strap it against your child's genitals, and do it again and again and again, you will soon see the tender skin redden and blister. These acid soaked cloths are commonly known as nappies, or diapers.

11. Let your child have several daily hours of fresh air and sunshine, and go naked as much as possible. Very small babies will need a layer of diapers underneath them if you do not wish to continually clean the floor, but what is the difference? You have to wash the diapers either way. This way your kids will be happy and healthy.

12. The human body is not sinful. It is beautiful, joyful, and can be pleasurable. It is not a sin to uncover it. It is a bad idea to cover your skin more than necessary. Because you are their example, this is especially true around children.

13. Water is also important. Bathe every day (more in summer), wash frequently, and swim all you can. The human is also a semi-aquatic animal, remember; and your soul needs water.

14. Make it a practice not to say "no" to your children unless you have to. Especially do not say no simply because the proposed activity involves noise or dirt.

15. You could almost say that getting dirty and making noise is a child's job. It is their job to learn and experiment and discover. You need to encourage this desire, not hinder it. Also try **very** hard not to keep the child from making mistakes. Fear of making a mistake will paralyze the child all their life.

16. A child will also learn neatness and cleanliness from you, if they learn it. Making a child aware of the responsibility for their own belongings simultaneous with awareness of possession will make it much easier from the start to instill a desire for an orderly environment.

17. If you pick up after a child until he is eight or ten, and then one day ask him to clean his room, he likely won't do it, regardless of bribe or threat. He **can't**, for he doesn't know how. You must let them

learn from the time they are capable of independent movement.

18. Likewise make care for their bodies part of awareness of their bodies. Explain what you are doing when you wipe their bottoms during a diaper change. Talk while you bathe them and wash their faces.

19. When a child comes in dirty from play, do not let anger show in your voice. Simply make it clear that to get clean afterward is an automatic part of playing and getting dirty.

20. Love and laughter will help your child learn anything you care to teach. Anger will only teach your child to fear you.

21. Never offer a bribe to a child. The difference between a bribe and a reward is when it is offered. The child must learn from the beginning that obedience to your requests is mandatory. The best way to teach this is positive behavior modification.

22. A child needs to learn to do what is required of him, needs to learn to do it willingly, and to do the best he can for his own sake. A small reward for doing his best is the best way to keep a child trying. Not every time or even most of the time, for then the child will begin to do the task for the sake of the reward.

23. Random positive reinforcement is by far the best way to buy "good" behavior.

# ∾Chapter 2∾

1.  There are two periods in a child's life when it may be advisable to use corporal punishment.

2.  Although using violence against another "for their own good" is always reprehensible, children can be like that famous mule: first you have to get their attention. But try to save the two-by-four as a last resort.

3.  A very small child needs to be taught not to eat or touch dangerous things. A loud handclap, close to the child, and a loud shout of "Danger!" should get their attention, and must be **immediately followed by an explanation.**

4.  This will train a child to stop whatever they are doing and turn to you for instructions.

5.  If you don't have enough imagination to see how valuable this practice will be throughout your child's life, perhaps you do not need to breed.

6.  It can even serve as a humorous opening to conversation when an older child wants to drive a car or to experiment with sex. And that can keep you from needing that old 2X4.

7.  Before you can give your child effective guidance into adulthood; such as listening to their fears about love, sex, and reproduction, you must first have a communication established with your child that allows the two of you to really talk.

8.  "Because I said so" is **never** an acceptable reason to give a child. You owe them an explanation. You will have to make it very simple for young children, but you must never omit it.

9.  If you have a good reason for everything you do, your child will trust you absolutely, and will continue throughout their lives to come to you for guidance.

10. You must always be prepared, of course, to change a "no" to a "yes" if the child has a better reason than you do. To be willing to change will teach the child many important things.

11. You are teaching the child that you respect his mind, and encouraging him, literally, to **reason** for himself.

12. If you cannot give a good reason for using compulsion toward a child you should not be doing it. Being willing to listen to your child is the most important developmental and training tool you can use, and you will also learn some very important things about yourself.

13. You may never need to know about the feel of worms underfoot or the taste of ants, but listening to your child, and responding on their level to what they say, will let your child know that she might

come to you when the 'taste' of her first sexual experience was not what she expected.

14. You know you have done a good job laying groundwork for honest communication when a child of the sex opposite yours confesses incestuous longings. Simply explain to the child why such feelings are natural but that acting on them can bring great tragedy; assure them that they are sexually desirable and are even more so to their own contemporaries.

15. Never express to a child, by word or tone or facial expression, that the child is bad to have had certain thoughts or questions. Instead impress upon the child that some thoughts **can not ever** become actions.

16. Most parents will have to spend a child's life trying frantically to stay one step ahead of the child's learning ability. Being prepared to answer any question reasonably and honestly will require you to be aware of your reasons for doing things, and honest with yourself about what those reasons are.

17. If you are unable or unwilling to make the effort to train a child properly, let us again suggest that you do not breed.

# ∽Chapter 3∽

1. There are three things that you can not tolerate from a child: tattling, whining, and defiance. Tolerating such behavior in children may lead to adults that behave in ways that require them to be killed.

2. A tattler should receive at least the punishment he intended that the culprit he told on should get. Whenever possible reinforce this by letting the culprit go free, difficult though it may be.

3. To praise and reward such an unhappy child does dreadful things to every child. It teaches children to buy pleasure at the price of another's pain, and it teaches them that the rules are more important than individuals. And worst of all, it teaches them **not** to mind their own business.

4. Only a person with a true hatred for life would want to demonstrate these things to innocent children: to the stool pigeon, to his victim, and to every other child in earshot. Do not encourage this sickness.

5.  Any other kind of emotional blackmail should be treated as what it is: an attempt at manipulating you through guilt, by a child who feels powerless.

6.  Teach a child that making a request politely phrased in an even tone increases the likelihood of the request being granted, while repeating the same demand with nothing but a change in pitch will close the discussion.

7.  Teach the child that a threat to turn blue will cause you to reach for a camera; and that running away from home will be met with an offer of stamps and stationery.

8.  Raising a child is a lifelong clash of wills. There is nothing you can do, except be prepared to laugh when there is nothing else you can do.

9.  You must be prepared to simulate losing an occasional battle. A child who learns that they can never win with you, will likely carry that feeling out into the world.

10. A child must learn early the difference between being assertive and aggressive. When a child's defiance becomes aggression, you **must** give them another lesson.

11. You have to get the child's attention, and if your signal doesn't deter immediately, a smack on the hand or bottom will help reinforce it. Never strike a small child anywhere else, and never with anything other than your hand.

12. However, you may find that you prefer an instrument of discipline with older children. A riding crop is ideal (because of the secondary connotations), but such things as a flyswatter or wooden spoon will serve.

13. You must never strike a child except to get their attention. Punishing a child physically, after an offense has occurred, is nothing but sadism; and causing a child to suffer fear of such a beating is inexcusable. **You have no right to ever threaten a child.**

14. Ideally the instrument of discipline is reserved for its designated use, kept in a prominent place, and replaced as needed. An intelligent child will need only one demonstration.

15. A child that says "no" to you in a calm voice, and clearly has a reason even if they cannot express it well, is already paying attention to you. There is a difference between opposition to your wishes, and defiance.

16. When a child loses their temper, the ability to reason will quickly follow. At that point you have two choices: you can lose **your** temper, or you can get their attention.

17. The instrument of discipline should be used to instruct, not to punish. When you feel yourself becoming emotionally involved in 'winning' an interchange with your child, and when you feel as if the child is challenging you, you may want to offer

them (and you!) a shortcut to regaining self control with a quick pop to the kid's flank.

18. Reaching for your riding crop will break a sequence of emotional escalation, and signal to your child that their behavior has gone out of bounds.

19. And feel free to bargain with your children, particularly when they wish to earn a privilege by assuming a responsibility. But you must never, ever bluff.

# ∼Chapter 4∼

1.  The amount of respect you earn from your children will be in direct proportion to how good is your word.

2.  Never break a promise to a child.

3.  A smart parent quickly realizes that this may mean trying not to make any promises at all; but that also applies to punishment.

4.  The first time you tell a child the penalty for an infraction, it is information. After that it is a threat. And for your sake and the child's, it must not be an empty one.

5.  You should always be open to mitigating circumstances, but generally not to pleas for mercy. Children can not become responsible adults unless they are consistently held to be accountable for their actions. If a child knows there is a specific punishment for a specific act, and chooses to perform that act, you owe it to the child to impose that penalty.

6.  Time-outs, loss of a privilege, a monetary fine or imposition of a chore: things like these are appropriate penalties for misbehavior. Corporal punishment is not, nor is using food to control the actions of a child.

7.  You may wish to use an occasional sweet treat as a
    spontaneous reward, but do not send your child to
    bed without supper as a punishment. Children who
    are taught to associate the pain of hunger with loss
    of love are being trained for later emotional prob-
    lems that only begin with obesity.

8.  There is, however, one instance where corporal
    punishment is entirely correct, and that is where
    there is intentional cruelty. Should you see a child
    hit, kick, or cause pain to an adult, animal, or
    another child, you must react at once. It may be dif-
    ficult for you to slap or pinch a child, or pull his
    hair; but receiving the identical pain is intended to
    grab the child's attention in a very specific way.

9.  This should be followed by a non-corporal punish-
    ment; plus a discussion as long and in-depth as the
    child can tolerate, so the child can understand how
    truly wrong it is to initiate violence against another.

10. A child must know not only why they are being
    punished; they should, as much as possible, know
    the reasons for everything that is done to them.

11. The habit of talking to your child can begin before
    birth, and if you are learning to listen while they are
    learning to speak, they will talk to you all their lives.

12. Love your children, teach them, play with them,
    and above all respect them. Look at them at least
    once a day with awe, just to remind you where they
    came from.

~Psongs, Book Two~

# Race to the Finish

# ~Chapter 1~

1. The last thing any government wants is for a citizen to escape state control.

2. Other than shows created for national pride, no government will ever send their citizens into space. The very thought, of someone going where there is no one to control him, is a thought to freeze the heart of a bureaucrat with terror.

3. There are three intelligent races on Earth, and if one of them 'wins' it will only be by default, through elimination of the other two. But if man can keep from poisoning his competition, he might soon have company.

4. There is a reason that every human oral history includes a tale of a world wide flood. It happened.

5. There are also many stories to account for the variety of human languages and appearances. These are also allegorically correct.

6. The new human race was humming right along, but we had perhaps found success a bit heady; and we

were eager to see what further attempts at polishing would accomplish.

7.  The change was a gentle one, this time: it warmed up a little, and the icecaps were melting, and it did rain. A lot. Not for weeks but for generations. And as the oceans rose and the land area shrank, humans moved to the high ground.

8.  Several major gene pools were largely isolated by the rising waters, and each made minor surface adaptations to local conditions. Those under the harshest conditions tended to breed the most competitive survivors, but this is their only distinction.

9.  Along with 'racial' variations, the rising and falling waters produced language diversity. The re-emerging groups met people who seemed far different from themselves. But one critical change did not happen.

10. There was a flightless bird on a Pacific island that managed to lose several offspring on another island nearby. They had no contact between islands, and the gene groups moved apart. In just a handful of years, the Great Auk and the Lesser Auk could no longer interbreed.

11. Many governments have laws to prevent breeding among people who lack perfect surface similarity. This alone should tip you off that mating between 'races' of man is highly desirable.

12. Humans can breed with neither dolphins nor apes. This is our intent. When and if we have a like desire (that those of dissimilar surface characteristics

remain genetically distinct), we can do a far better job of arranging it than can you.

13. There are Great Auks and Lesser Auks, but there are no White humans or Red humans, or black or yellow; and though we feel there is a distinction between humans and Humanettes; for the time being, we will give the Humans a chance to rid themselves of the Humanettes.

14. But no promises! Repent while you can, those of you who hate the life we have given you. Do not hate yourself, or your own life. Most especially, do not try to keep others from being happy simply because you are not.

# ∾Chapter 2∾

1. God and government **always** agree on at least one thing: hate is a most marketable commodity.

2. The peculiar situation of one religious group choosing only to breed with their own, and thereby creating their own sub-race, was an experiment we had no hand in designing; and though the results have been instructive, they do not bode entirely well for future human happiness.

3. These folks represent many of the things humans were designed to be, though not necessarily by their own conscious design. We heartily approve of a tradition that mandates choosing the best available breeding combinations, but the other factors in the success of these people are more tragic.

4. They are nomadic, and they are frequently culled by their fellow man.

5. Governments in trouble have been trying to 'blame it on the Jews' almost as long as there have been Jewish people, and with regrettably regular success.

6.  These good folk tend to habitually display the classic invitation to hatred—they mind their own business—and they have an extra fault, one which can inspire even more rage. Many of them tend to be successful.

7.  To create superior characteristics in a given gene pool, breed to reinforce your desired objectives and cull heavily those which do not meet your standard. Throughout history rulers have tried to deflect people's outrage onto scapegoats, and have often persuaded their subjects that they can better their own lives by killing their Jewish neighbors.

8.  Hundreds of generations of careful inbreeding and spasmodic culling have given the world an example of what humanity can be. Do not be jealous of them; try instead to be like them. Mind your own business.

9.  It is entirely natural to greet the unknown with fear and curiosity. It is entirely unnatural, for any being, to greet the unknown with fear and hatred. For a human to hate at all is not part of the design; hate must be taught.

10. God/vernments will always find a scapegoat for you to hate. It is essential for them to always force your focus away from themselves; and if your anger cannot be turned back on you, they must direct it elsewhere. If a religious or racial minority is not handy, another target will be manufactured. It is the official policy of every church and every ruler that you have someone to blame for your problems.

11. The races of man were created as part of the effort to find out how far humanity **could** go, not how far it **would** go.

# ∼Chapter 3∼

1. You may go anywhere you can get to; but don't wait for your government to send you there.

2. Assuming you no longer believe in fairy tales or the benevolence of your god or government, it is equally unwise to anticipate serious state development of space. It will not happen in our lifetimes.

3. The possibility of development is there, as long as government offers no interference. The people who invest early in space exploration will have very grateful grandchildren, for there are unimagined fortunes waiting just beyond the stratosphere.

4. The spate of affirmative action laws produced by the American Congress in the *1960*'s was a response by that body when they were threatened with the loss of their favorite minority.

5. Really, it was unbelievable—asking to ride on a bus, drink from a fountain, learn at school—something had to be done, but quick! Before these people could actually achieve equality for themselves, 'their' gov-

ernment rushed to the rescue with several thousand pages of meaningless legal mumbo-jumbo.

6. This government is composed of the people who will lead the human race into space? Perhaps you should not withhold respiration in anticipation of that event.

7. Colonization is a process whereby the disease takes over and finally becomes the host. Now that the world has grown so short of native peoples to enslave and exploit, new lands appear to have lost appeal for the ruling classes.

8. Anyone who sneers at 'the profit motive' deserves to be slapped, but our ethics forbid suggesting the initiation of violence. Jealousy aside, space will have to be developed by those with an economic stake in it, if man is to reach the stars. And you will likely find it most educational to visit some of our other laboratories.

9. The traditional image of the pioneer is the tough, two-fisted conqueror of the plains; the one with his courageous wife at his shoulder and brood of stalwart sons just behind. Out there in the wilderness where there is no one to say yea or nay; where a man lives with his wits and dies with his failures; where a man can enjoy his own vine and fig tree, with none to make him afraid.

10. Obviously that "none" includes lawyers, tax collectors, and administrators of social programs.

11. Quite by accident, some government policies are helping lead public thought in exactly the direction the gods would wish you to go: children now growing up will know, without being told, that everyone can go into space.

12. Although Affirmative Action is actually designed to hinder the people it is supposed to help, it has caused several governments to place 'show' minority representation in their 'show' space programs.

13. Many countries are seeking out the most qualified scientists from among the minority populations within their borders. The inescapable message they are bearing to the world is that the best and the brightest, the most special among you, come in all shapes and colors; and that ability is more important than appearance.

14. Humanity was divided into separate races for two reasons. We were attempting to perfect several strains at the same time; and the crude shaping tools thus far used, which were planet-wide, could be refined by localizing extremes. So it saved everybody time to run several experiments at once.

15. The other reason was the possibility of still more genetic gain, promised by the prospect of re-mixing the newly produced varieties. This is the reason humans have always, without regard to minor surface differences, and always will, remain capable of interbreeding.

16. Governments might, out of a deep fear of any person escaping control, manage to keep the human race confined to their planet of origin. But if men and women do make it into space, we are most pleased that you will do it our way.

# ∾Chapter 4∾

*1.* Meanwhile do not expect "intelligence" from another planet to land and ask for your **leaders**.

## ~Psongs, Book Three~

# Eat, Drink and Be Very

# ~Chapter 1~

1.  Be very wary of what you eat and drink.

2.  Most people have been grossly misinformed about food. Your health and appearance should be the result of planning, not luck.

3.  If there is one dietary commandment, it is Thou Shall Not Over-Eat.

4.  The human stomach is designed to be satisfied with 200 to 300 calories at a time, and about twice that amount will provide a comfortable fullness.

5.  Gorging yourself with 20 to 30 times the amount you need is most unwise. Were you to ingest twenty times the customary dosage of any other drug—such as aspirin, or alcohol—in the same amount of time, the results would usually be fatal. Since digestion is one of the body's two most important functions, you may wish to learn to work with it.

6.  The first thing you need to know is that your body wants to be healthy; and it will cooperate vigorously with any steps you take in that direction.

7.  The second is that most people eat a diet of pure garbage.

8.  Start every day with at least two or three servings of fresh juicy fruit. As the morning progresses and your hunger grows, try adding apples, raisins, bananas, and nuts. Try to nibble, and stop after a handful of the more concentrated foods. Freshly squeezed fruit juices are also excellent.

9.  Fresh vegetables, lightly steamed with a bit of butter or raw with a dip; along with salads lightly dressed, and whole grains; these will satisfy mid-day hungers well. Freshly juiced vegetables, such as carrot or cucumber, are liquid energy.

10.  Save your heaviest meal for last.

11.  Try not to combine starch with protein. Animal protein is the most difficult food for humans to digest, and you do it at different speeds and with different digestive juices than you need for starches.

12.  Your stomach is designed to best digest small portions of a single food, and combining all "four food groups" in a single meal is simply idiotic. For one thing, you must eat far too much to accomplish this.

13.  Eating food improperly causes improper digestion. Food that cannot be digested must be removed from the stomach in another manner.

14.  A dog that eats of something inedible will simply vomit; a horse that does so usually dies. But the human digestive system is more complex.

15. Never eat fresh fruit with any other food, and never eat it unless your stomach is empty. Do not combine any two proteins together, nor should you eat animal protein and starch in the same meal.

16. Each food has its own digestive acids, and mixing them together will impair or completely prevent digestion. Food that cannot be digested must stay in your stomach until it rots.

17. The toxic residue of this chemical breakdown is then extracted from the stomach via the bloodstream; and if you are lucky, it is eliminated from the body.

18. However, your body can only eliminate so much toxic material each day, and what cannot be eliminated must be stored in your body. To isolate this material, the body encapsulates each molecule in water; this is then stored in such places as your hips, buttocks, and thighs.

19. Severely obese people can easily lose a pound a day by simply eating **with** their bodies, instead of eating against their own natural rhythms.

20. Fresh fruit is pure energy; the more of it you eat, the more energy your body has to flush out stored toxins. Raw vegetables are also highly recommended; together, fresh fruits and vegetables should comprise at least three quarters of the calories you consume.

21. The body has four major elimination organs, (mouth, skin, bladder, and bowel), and you may notice changes in each when you begin eating prop-

erly. Changes in bowel and bladder habits are to be expected when those organs suddenly begin to function better, and keeping your skin and mouth a little cleaner will take care of residues left by the cleansing process.

22.  We have provided good stuff for you; please use it.

# ∽Chapter 2∼

1.  You also have good bodies. Use them, damn it!

2.  Lots of sex is good for you. So is running, jumping, and singing. Laughter is wonderful, as is dancing.

3.  Your bodies are made to be used. Many ills of the body are caused by not getting enough exercise; many others are caused by too much of one kind of exercise.

4.  A balanced life of action and rest and periods of thought and meditation will help maintain a balanced mind. A body should stretch and sweat and breathe hard several times a day; a mind should do the same. Reward yourself throughout with laughter and play whenever possible.

5.  A body fit in mind and body must be a fit body. Eating well is only half the job. If you are not in the habit of at least a small daily workout, you will balance the unhappiness this brings to your life by making that life shorter.

6.  Do not overeat, and try not to underexercise.

7. Making a resolution to begin exercising an hour a
   day is dangerous to your health and doomed to failure. If you truly wish to change your lifestyle, do it in
   small steps.

8. It is not recommended, unless you are excessively
   fond of cervical collars, that you ever lock your fin-
   gers behind your head and yank sharply forward.
   There are dozens of better ways to work your abdom-
   inal muscles.

9. But whether you choose a healthier form of situps,
   or pick pushups, or squat-thrusts, or deep knee
   bends, very few people can commit to a crash program and carry through with it.

10. To change your habits for life, start small. Do one,
    or three, or five pushups. Or situps or whatever.
    This is a commitment anyone can keep, and
    requires neither large investment nor lots of time.
    (Start small!)

11. Your body will respond by immediately asking for
    more, but keep it at a level that you can do without
    hesitation every day.

12. It is more important to do a little each day than to
    do a lot every now and then. And every day it will
    become easier to do, and will actually become
    enjoyable, in a way.

13. Keep increasing your workout; but be secure at each
    level before moving on to the next, and drop back to
    your previous level if you find yourself slacking off.

14. Eating right and exercising will quickly take your body to its natural weight. Learn to distinguish between eating to fuel your body and eating to feed your emotions.

15. Stop eating when you have eaten enough to satisfy your present hunger. The first time you reach for a liquid, to cleanse your palate; or the first time, after you have begun to eat, that you reach for a condiment such as salt; these are signals that you have eaten all you need, and you should eat no more at that time.

16. Do not be alarmed if this happens after only a few bites. That is all your stomach is designed to hold.

17. Make it a habit to carry a pocket toothbrush, and an ironclad rule to use it every time you eat **anything**. Mega-benefits: you will finish eating before others in social settings, so just excuse yourself for a moment. If you brush your teeth, you won't take "just one more bite" after you sit down again. And you won't try to kid yourself about having just **one** cookie or chip.

18. And this practice makes it easier to resist those who would force you to eat because it makes them feel less fat. (Ever see a skinny person insist that you eat, when they know you are trying to diet?) (Thanks, but I just brushed my teeth.) And finally, just think about the lack of dental bills!

19. Forget a scale if you want to get into shape. No artificially set number will tell you the state of your

health like a full length mirror; if necessary, eat nude in front of it.

20. Look at your body often, and praise each success you achieve. Resolve to try harder on the morrow if you should happen to slip.

21. Above all, enjoy your body. That is what it is for.

# Definitive Testament:
# Non Carborundum Illegitimati

## Book Nine

# Real Men Don't Eat Crap (Real Women Don't, Either)

# ∼Chapter 1∼

1.  Your life is worth less to your government than cows' farts.

2.  A half million dollars to investigate bovine methane emissions may not sound like much. However, several people will have to work and pay taxes all their lives to create that much money.

3.  It can only be that you tolerate such madness because that is how little you value your own life; if it is only because you have been heretofore ignorant of the true nature of your servitude, pay heed.

4.  Never doubt that you are government property. The laws everywhere prohibiting suicide are proof enough of that. But a free people can be enslaved when they fail to see the nature of their chains.

5.  The Government Does Not Exist For Your Benefit. Rulers everywhere, always, operate wholly and solely for the benefit of rulers. You are a cipher: your job is to work, to pay, and to do as you are told.

6.  The United States government, in particular, has made itself virtually revolution-proof: an armed

uprising is unlikely when over half of the population receives the majority of their support from the ever willing (and ever diminishing!) American taxpayer.

7.  Civil servants and retirees, especially those who collect a pension after 'retiring' from 'public office;' justice industry employees, from cops to janitors to jailers; public utility workers and garbage collectors; public school teachers and administrators; the list of those who root from the public trough is endless.

8.  Also unlikely to bite the hand that writes the checks are those who receive Social Security or military pensions.

9.  The government's record of ruining whatever it touches is going to remain intact as long as people continue to tolerate intrusion, invasion, and interference. The rules and regulations that govern every single moment of your life, if printed in books and piled in a stack, would reach to the moon.

10. Not only does this confusing, contradictory, and all-pervasive mess of 'laws' threaten you with imprisonment or impoverishment for any false step; but someone has to write, edit, collate, publish, and **administer** all those "for your own good" rules.

11. It is also, of course, for your own good that you pay for the boon of such (ad)ministration.

# ∼Chapter 2∼

1. According to some, everyone has a right to:
   Food
   Housing
   Medical care
   Clothing
   Transportation
   Education
   Employment
   This is a very peculiar notion.

2. Making such a demand with the government behind you means you wish to be able to force those who work to provide such things for you, on pain of death.

3. Lust does not give you the right to rape, no more than does rain give you the right to steal an umbrella. Being unable to feed yourself only gives you the right to starve.

4. Mankind did not invent welfare—many creatures care for their own young, old, and injured—but he did create the bizarre practice of forcing others to pay for the luxury of his own pity. You cannot get to heaven by paying for your compassion with other

people's money, and if you try to do it with money taken by force, you can go straight to hell.

5.  That three babies are born every second should occasion joy; but when they come into the world with the prospect of forcing their fellow man to satisfy their every whim, the taxpayers usually do not celebrate.

6.  The definition of a 'right' has become terribly confused; but a 'right' is only one thing. The first ten amendments to the American Constitution are usually called the "Bill of Rights," and each amendment specifies something the government **may not do** to its citizens. **A right is an immunity,** no more and no less.

7.  You do indeed have many rights to keep others from interfering with you. You do not have the right to make forcible demands of strangers.

8.  The phrase "a right to...(medical care, housing, etc.)" is **always** verbal shorthand for the reality of the words. Expressing that you have 'a right' to a material benefit of any kind **always** means that you think you have "a right to force others to provide" that benefit.

9.  You do not have the right to require a person to go through the arduous and expensive years of medical school; then offer their professional skills to you for free, just because you perceive that you have a 'need' for a doctor's care.

10.  A carpenter working to build a house does this work so he can bring home a paycheck and feed his family. He does not wish to work for free so that you can

have a home that you are unwilling to earn. Likewise the contractor buys the lumber and shingles, and hires the carpenter to build the house, so that it can be sold to pay for the cost of its construction.

11. They do not wish to hand over this house to people who will break the windows, punch holes in the walls, and piss in the corners; and then demand another free house when they have made the first uninhabitable.

12. A 'progressive' income tax appears to be progress only on the road to destruction. This is **nothing** but a penalty on ability and hard work, and can only be intended to discourage work; since the U. S. government is quite vocal about their habit of taxing that which they wish to discourage, and subsidizing behaviors the government wishes to encourage.

13. Therefore by punishing hard work and subsidizing helplessness, your government is clearly telling you that they prefer you to be ~~hopeless~~ helpless.

14. The plight of welfare mothers is generally explained by two ancient shibboleths: lack of job skills and prohibitively expensive day care. **Who is kidding whom?**

15. Accepting a government check for the care of dependent children is an implicit claim that you are qualified to care for children. Therefore every person on welfare is immediately employable. The desperate need for child care should mean a job for all.

16. Those who administer and inspect welfare programs will of course be against any improvement in the lot of those they 'help.' They will shut up if

offered jobs administering and inspecting day-care facilities instead.

17. Instead of handing out cash, provide those who wish to work with day care. Those who cannot find jobs in the private sector will do the day care for those that work; and instead of a monthly check, every person can be employed in the day care centers. Those workers will of course take their own children to work with them. The transition to a free and self supporting lifestyle must begin with the concept that **everybody works**.

18. Elaborate facilities are not needed: a center could be started with no up front money, and you would soon see some apartment buildings with one on every floor. The price of maintaining one family in public housing for a year would easily pay for child care for a dozen working families.

19. And the money would be spent teaching people independence instead of how to be dependent. Which is why it will not be done.

# ∼Chapter 3∼

1.  When the government takes all your money so it can give you "free" things, just remember this:

2.  Anything free is worth what you pay for it.

3.  If government were to magically disappear this morning, by nightfall every essential service would be voluntarily offered to the public, usually at greater efficiency and lower cost. Any services not so offered can be deemed to be considered unnecessary by the public. Where there is a need, there is usually a profit.

4.  The services that were not privatized or cooperatively organized would be the ones for which the public is obviously unwilling to pay. Those who would insist that **you** pay for what **they** think you need (or want you to need, which is often the case), should be invited to demonstrate the depth of their commitment to fulfilling your needs.

5.  Invite them to pay for it.

6.  Attention all liberals: the day of the death cult is done. If getting your name in the paper for whining

about 'equality' makes you feel important, you will probably keep on sniveling; but do not try to kid yourself. If you truly cared about **anything** outside yourself, you would try to find something positive to do about it, and you certainly are not fooling anyone else about your true beliefs.

7. Forget 'the poor' until they ask for your help. When someone tells you that they themself are in need, you are encouraged to assist that person to the limit of your resources. Do not annoy people who have not asked for your intervention by trying to convince them of their needs.

8. If you are indeed one of these fouled souls, you have a very warped view of what people 'need' anyway. Glorifying the worst within you to seek a value in your own life, while pretending to help those less fortunate, is a pitiful effort to hide your own inner inadequacy. By projecting the lack of material things in the lives of others onto the absence of any value in your own life, you can escape the emptiness of your own soul for a while.

9. Of course it will only be for a while; and like anyone addicted to a corrosive habit, you will need repeated and larger doses to get your sanctimony fix. Your biggest fear is that the poor actually **will** learn to help themselves, and your absolute worthlessness will be finally exposed beyond all denial.

10. And while you are busy buying gratitude by dispensing your extorted bounty, do you ever spare even a

moment of compassion for the poor hard-working slob from whom that money has been stolen?

11. Robin Hood **did not** steal from the rich to give to the poor!

12. The first inkling most of the American public gained of the aborted rescue mission to Teheran in *1980*, to rescue the Americans held captive in the American Embassy, was the newsflash detailing the Pentagon's statement: that there had not been, nor would there be, a rescue attempt. Oddly enough, at the moment this denial was issued, there were three Army helicopters flaming on the desert floor.

13. Do Not Trust 'Your' Government. **They Lie.**

14. The government-approved version of the legend of Sherwood Forest is that of a band of outlaws, robbing innocent citizens and using some of the proceeds to bribe the local peasantry into silence.

15. In actuality, the Earl of Locksley 'robbed' the IRS, and returned the money to its rightful owners.

16. Think about it.

## Book Ten

# The Money Tree

# ❧Chapter 1❧

1. Money does indeed grow on trees.

2. 'Money' can be anything of value: it is not limited to that funny paper stuff your government prints.

3. In the United States, it costs more to buy the paper and print a dollar bill than a dollar will actually buy. This is why that government tried replacing the bill with a coin a few years ago.

4. Of course, you were told neither the real reason for its introduction nor why it was suddenly thereafter dropped.

5. One-dollar coins were only minted for a short time before it was discovered that they cost more to produce than the bills. One would think this factor might have been considered beforehand; but what is a few billion of the taxpayer's money anyway?

6. If you have ever wondered why Congress throws money away like it was toilet paper, perhaps it is because they know something you do not.

7.  There appear to be three basic types of human economy. Barter; and the hunter/gatherer type, wherein everyone basically fends for themself; cannot stretch enough to fit the needs of modern man. The third type is where everyone agrees to use a universal symbol of value.

8.  A symbol of value should be stable. Fruit grown on the trees has a value and can be exchanged for other things of value; but it is not stable, because it decays and loses value.

9.  Many cultures have used such things as shells and slices of animal tusk to represent a standard of value. Many now use precious metals.

10. Silver and gold especially make excellent symbols of value. They are easily divisible, do not react readily with other substances, and are usually somewhat difficult to acquire. Metal coinage has one big drawback, however: it is easy to dilute its value without anyone noticing.

11. Were you to melt down a silver coin, and add enough tin or lead to make two coins, you would be counterfeiting. When a government does this to a large number of coins at once, this counterfeiting is legal. It is called inflation.

12. Hard money is bulky, and can be dangerous to transport. The first paper money was a pledge carried by a traveler, to be redeemed in gold at the city of his arrival. This method quickly caught on, and

soon clearing houses appeared where any traveler could exchange a pledge for money.

13. Another form of counterfeiting is writing a pledge when you do not have the corresponding amount of gold on deposit. This is also called inflation when done by a government.

14. A "banknote" is a pledge that the issuer of the note has sufficient precious metals on hand to redeem that note for the amount of metal promised on the face. To tender such a false note is theft, even when done by a government.

# ~Chapter 2~

1. Forcing the legal tender laws onto the populace was a critical component in the takeover of the American economy.

2. The difference between a dollar bill which is worth a specified amount of silver, and a dollar bill that is worth whatever the government claims it is worth, is that the former is the currency of a free people.

3. Unfortunately, the money in the 'land of the free' is worth absolutely nothing.

4. This is a currency backed by neither gold nor silver, or even the fruit off the trees. If you read the small print, a dollar is backed instead by the "full faith and credit" of the government that was denying the deaths of its servicemen while their bodies were still smoking. That is their faith: their credit is based on **admitting** that they (you!) are several trillion dollars in debt.

5. This is on a par with calling the tax system 'voluntary.' People do indeed pay willingly; because the alternative is torture, imprisonment, or death. If

you do not believe they will kill you for not paying your taxes, try it. If you do survive the experience, you may well wish you had not.

6.  The 16th Amendment to the U. S. Constitution permitted the government to impose a tax on incomes. It was never ratified by a sufficient number of states, but the Congress enacted it anyway, because 'the government' needed the money. But according to their own rules it is not legal.

7.  Taking money you have no right to, by making threats against people that have the right to the money, is called extortion.

8.  A truly voluntary tax system would allow each citizen to decide how much they wish to contribute, and what kinds of spending they wish to support. Instead of giving a line-item veto to the President, why not give the veto power to the people who are actually earning the money which will be spent?

9.  A simple checkoff form will permit each person to indicate how much they wish to contribute. A person who favors a strong national defense can pay all of their taxes to the military; a person who wishes the government to help the poor may donate all of their income, if they so wish, to finance such help.

10. Being unable to support oneself does not confer the right to force others to support one. A government unable to pay for itself is not granted the right of using extortion to garner spending money.

11. Taxation is theft, and whether it is import or corporate or personal income taxes, it is all being stolen from you.

12. Any government that will waste the lives of its citizens on cows' farts has too much money to spend. The governors would quickly lose interest in caring for their pets if money stolen from others were not available to pay for that care. And hammers and toilet seats, when needed, should be purchased at a competitive price.

13. If the government does have a legitimate need for cash, lotteries and the sale of non-monopolistic services are but a few of the methods available for raising voluntary contributions.

14. In fact, it makes the most elegant kind of sense, that if someone wants to **spend** money, they should be required to **raise** that money.

# ⌒Chapter 3⌒

1. The first American revolution was fought over gun control.

2. The colonists appeared prepared to tolerate, with symbolic resistance at best, any outrage the British cared to perpetrate. They didn't shoot back until British troops marched upon the arms that were stored at Concord. The revolution started over the right to be armed.

3. It is rather obvious that when the Founding Fathers referred to the rights of humanity regarding the overthrow of tyrants, they had no intention that the right be limited to tyrannies of the **past**.

4. Do not misinterpret that! We **are not** recommending the violent overthrow of any government. We would much prefer you simply ignore the government until it goes away; but it is an excellent idea to remind the government, on every possible occasion, that it does not have the right to prevent its own dismissal.

5. This is of course the terror (that their true natures will be made public) of every parasite. Take care

never to threaten such creatures unless absolutely necessary. For example, it is most unwise to inform any minion of the tax terror brigade that there is no legal requirement you pay federal income taxes.

6.  Be warned! Any attempt to enforce the 'right' (correct usage!) to keep any person or agency from taking your money will subject you to persecution from the IRS that a Spanish Inquisitor would envy.

7.  The year *1965* saw yet another blow to freedom in America. Believe it or not, the justification for their replacing silver coins with alloy replicas was as follows: Since pay telephones and parking meters were designed to accept certain sized coins, those sizes and shapes must be maintained, even if it meant destroying the monetary value of those coins. Thus the 'sandwich' coin was born.

8.  A U. S. Quarter does not contain twenty-five cents worth of silver, not when silver is selling for around *$5.00* per ounce. You were told that the 'sandwich' coins would have enough silver to make the coins worth their face value, but they do not. These coins are as counterfeit as if you had made them in your basement, and the U. S. Constitution specifically forbids government counterfeiting; but since real silver coins were last being minted, quite a few phony coins have somehow come into circulation.

9.  Control a being's economy and you control the being. They have so far either been too smart, or too stupid (you choose), to go in a big way for your guns.

10. They **have** gotten your money. Will you wait until it is too late?

*Book Eleven*

# Pity the Poor,
# Diseased Politician

# ∾Chapter 1∾

1.  And the little boy said, "But he has no clothes!"

2.  And the Emperor's guard surrounded the boy, and clubbed him to death with their rifle butts...and no one else wanted to speak, and so the parade went on....

3.  Your Congress spends 95% of their time taking money from one place and apportioning it elsewhere. The rest of their time they spend giving you such good things as Dental Health Month and National Frozen Food Week.

4.  Perhaps they would have less time to interfere in the lives of their subjects if people required politicians to raise the money that they are so fond of spending.

5.  There is a plot afoot to fasten the yoke even tighter to your shoulders. As usual, their mouth is busy assuring you how much you 'need' this improvement, while their hands are busy unzipping their collective fly. A Constitutional Amendment to Balance the Budget is a law forcing Congress to raise your taxes every time they wish to spend money.

6. Can't you hear the wails from Washington even now? "But we **have** to raise your taxes! It's the **law!**"

7. And you are supposed to believe that this will cause them to LIMIT their spending!!

8. Instead, they should be given carte blanche to spend all they wish; as long as they raise the money **without coercion.**

9. In order to be elected President, a person must be born in the United States. The only other eligibility requirement for any elected office is attaining the specified number of years. A politician need not qualify by means of temperament, training, or education; perhaps no one cares whether or not they are capable of performing the duties of office because most chimpanzees could perform those duties with equal skill?

10. However, the fact that breathing in and out enough times is all it takes to be voted in, is matched by making sufficient respirations the only qualification needed to do the voting.

11. The framers of the American Constitution never intended to place the power of the franchise in irresponsible hands. Possession of a warm body was not considered at the time to qualify a person as a decision-maker: a voter was required to first be someone with a demonstrated stake in the wellbeing of the community. One could qualify by owning a farm or business, or by being engaged as a journeyman at his trade.

12. In other words, only a taxpayer was entitled to decide who should spend his tax money. Perhaps the belief that unqualified voters will make poor decisions is the reason politicians lend such enthusiastic support to giving the vote to everyone.

13. If you feel you must have rulers, there are many ways to select them that do not involve popularity contests. The best among such ways would also supply the government with income; and of these ways, the auction formats will bring other positive results.

14. Recently a man ran for a Senate seat in a western state on a 'platform' that consisted of photographs of aborted fetuses with his name superimposed on the film. Rather than subjecting an unsuspecting public to such sickening garbage, why not require candidates to contribute those funds to the operating budget of the territory they wish to rule?

15. That would be one method for choosing public servants: the office will go to the candidate who deposits the most money in the government coffers. Losing candidates would not receive a refund.

16. The general collective wisdom is that an election always goes to the one who spends the most money. Instead of mud-slinging ads and all the foolish attempts at campaign reform, voters might prefer having the process made open and aboveboard.

17. A slightly different approach would have similar results. A voter could buy as many votes as they liked, to cast for the candidate of their choice. The

entire Federal income would be contributed voluntarily, by those who felt strongly enough about the
outcome of the election to put up hard-earned
money. The President and Congressmen would be
those who received the most cash votes.

18. Though there are many ways to make elections
more honest, there is no known way to make a
**politician** honest.

# ∽Chapter 2∽

1. You should indeed feel sorry for your politicians, for they are the saddest of the sad.

2. Imagine a being so empty inside that you live only for the lives of others, for the chance to control those lives. This can only be done by those who feel their own life has no worth.

3. Try to understand the envy and hatred they feel when they look at you, when they see you living and enjoying your own a life and they know they cannot have what you have. Knowing that they do not deserve a happy life, their goal becomes the equality of universal unhappiness.

4. It is unclear just why the American medical industry had the recent emergency; when people go there from all over the world for their care. The actual 'crisis' was a politician with absolutely nothing to offer the public. He needed a fear campaign, so that people would then require the services of this politician in guiding massive government intervention to solve the crisis, which crisis **did not exist**

before he tried to frighten the people he claimed to want to serve!

5.  Consider whether you really need leaders, if this is all they have to offer you.

6.  Anarcho-capitalism is the political and economic portion of the philosophy of KYFHO. It is the belief that if a man is left free to benefit himself, others will automatically benefit from his actions. There aren't very many that are free to benefit themself nowadays.

7.  Every ballot ought to offer "none of the above" as a choice for each office. If "no one" receives the most votes, obviously the public wishes none of the available candidates to have the office. Or else they do not wish the office to exist.

8.  However, voicing this observation aloud may well subject you to assassination by a politician; for they will kill as many as they need to, to keep you from realizing that **you don't need them.**

9.  Your life does not require a comptroller of cunnilingus or a drug czar or a pointless politician forcing health insurance upon you. You do not need a leech with a gun to take most of your daily wage on the pretext that someone else is more 'entitled' to your money than are you.

10. Social security recipients are entitled to receive a reasonable return on their investment, especially as that investment is made at gunpoint. The problem is, from whom will the money come?

11. The Social Security system is based on the premise that you are too stupid and lazy to provide for your own future, so you must be forced to pay now so that you will not suffer later. (Why does that sound so much like a church?) The theme is always the same: you must be protected from your own decisions **for your own good**.

12. So the country was gifted with a 'retirement' crisis, much like the recent health care crisis; with the goal of creating a whole new bureaucracy. If they had actually wanted to 'help' those who were destined to become the elderly poor, it would have been much simpler to pass a law requiring each person to maintain a retirement savings account. But the government will never use guidance where force can be enjoyed.

13. If a minimum wage worker were to place five percent of their earnings in a simple savings account over the course of their working life, they could retire with around a million dollars in the bank. They could live generously as long as they wished on the interest, and then pass on the million, intact, to their grandchildren.

14. Since Social Security cannot quite match that, why not make it optional? If the government wishes to insist you provide for your future, you should at least be given the choice of where you invest your money.

15. Until then, as more and more people try to live on the miserable pittance doled out as their 'entitled' return, stock in pet food companies will become an ever better investment.

# ∽Chapter 3∽

1. In the same fashion, part of the takeover of the American economy was justified by the 'bank failure crisis.'

2. In simple terms, people were bringing money in the door of the bank, where it was promptly thrown out the window; and when they asked for their money back, it was not there.

3. The 'retirement' crisis and the 'bank failure crisis' could have been solved simultaneously with a minimum of intervention, **had those crises actually existed**. But they were pure invention. Nothing happened. There was no crisis.

4. There was definitely economic dislocation. The creation of the Federal Reserve gave the government the power to literally **print** money; that is, to create artificial symbols of value and claim that these symbols actually represented something. Giving itself the power to spend that printed toilet paper and force people to accept it, as if it was real money, caused such massive economic disruption, the entire country began to come apart at the seams.

5.  Money is the glue that holds a modern society together, and as they watered the money down, the society began to dissolve. That is what caused the bank failures, the stock market crash, and the Great Depression.

6.  Throughout the *1920*'s, government printing presses put their phony money into circulation **each year,** in amounts equaling up to ten percent of the total money in circulation. **Every year!!**

7.  Did it not occur, to even one soul, that suddenly turning off that tap just might cause things to dry up a bit?

8.  The "money-supply rate" measures how much artificial currency the government will pump into the economy this year. To simplify it for a minute, suppose there is a million dollars now in circulation; in bank vaults and cash registers, in people's wallets and piggy banks. If the money-supply figure for the year is ten percent, that means the government will print one hundred thousand dollars and spend them as if they were real money. (There is much more money than that in circulation, of course. This is a simplified example.)

9.  After a decade and a half of dumping ever increasing amounts of funny money into unsuspecting public hands, the government stopped the presses cold. In July of *1928* the money supply figure was at *10.2*%. In October of that year it was reported at zero.

10. Though the stock market crash was the gaudiest aftereffect of that idiocy, the depression actually started within weeks of the halt in the money pump, and was well under way before the shock waves finally hit Wall Street. This time the egg came before the chicken: it was the depression that caused the banks to fail, and the markets to crash.

11. And it was the government that caused the depression.

12. We do not know if it was genius or sheer stupidity that caused the Chairman of the Federal Reserve to do such an incredibly destructive thing (a toddler with an atomic weapon comes to mind), but the results of that action are as clear as they were catastrophic.

13. Government control of the economy is good for you.

14. Really.

# ~Chapter 4~

1. Money is power; and if you are a politician, other people's money means your power.

2. Therefore politicians want as much of your money as they can grab.

3. A thug with a gun operates on the premise that he can spend your money better than you can. So does the government. The difference is that the thug does not tell you that robbery is for your own good. The government does.

4. When an oil tanker ran aground in Alaska a few years ago, it spilled a quarter million barrels of crude oil, fouling the waters and beaches and killing large numbers of animals, birds and fish. The American government responded promptly to the tragedy.

5. The U. S. Fish and Game Department proved how vital is the service it provides by spending almost a million dollars in Prudhoe Bay, to kill still more birds and animals.

6. This was done with **your** tax money, for your own good.

7.  It is not clear exactly how slaughtering distant wildlife is to your benefit, but you turn over huge chunks of your money because the government can spend it better than you can. Or at least they intend to try; and will continue to forcibly collect a 'tax' on your income, even though by their own rules it is not legal for them to do so.

8.  It is hard to imagine a thief using your money so stupidly. Why do you want people to rule you at all, if they cannot even match a common street thug for smarts?

9.  It is not easy to single out one human practice as more idiotic than others, but there is a real belly laugh situation developing whenever elected officials give themselves a raise. They assume that, as long as they are stealing such great gobs of your money anyway, you will not mind if a little more of that money goes directly into their own pockets. Obviously, you do not mind; because they do it with great regularity.

10. The Federal Minimum Wage is designed to give everyone who works enough money upon which to live. Even though your elected officials do not do productive work, many people feel an obligation to pay something to your President and Congressmen for suiting up and showing up. If so, it is fair that they should receive enough to live on. There is **no** earthly reason they should have more than they think is enough for you. Is there?

11. Do you really feel sympathetic when they snivel about how hard they work to steal and waste your money?

12. Judge their intentions by their actions. If you have never read the Federal Budget, you are ignorant of the true intent of your rulers.

13. Politicians will keep the concept of 'the divine right of kings' a reality as long as you let them; but there is no reason in heaven either, that a Congressman should vote to pay himself a couple hundred thousand dollars a year of **your** money.

14. Short version: "I didn't inhale."

15. Long version: "I did something I knew was wrong; not because I wanted to do it, but because I was afraid of what people would think of me if I didn't. And by pretending I was one of them when I was not, I cheated them, too." (And exactly how did you "try" it, if you didn't inhale? Snorting it? Injecting it? Or suppository? No wonder you didn't like it!)

16. Congratulations on your election, Mr. President. You certainly deserved it. But, did they?

~Book Twelve~

# The Year They
# Shot the Lawyers….

# ~Chapter 1~

1. ...and the tax collectors, politicians, preachers, and pitchmen....

2. You may not, however, engage in wholesale slaughter, **no matter how good** your reasons may seem.

3. Prostitutes, murderers and thieves were welcomed in the American colonies; but for the first forty years not one settlement would allow a lawyer to land on their shores. They were considered too troublesome, too likely to cause quarrels among their neighbors.

4. Ladies and gentlemen, those pioneers were on to something.

5. This is a profession that touts a total lack of moral conviction as 'ethics.' No wonder your laws are difficult for the ordinary citizen to understand: give us an honest prostitute any day. Part of the process of legal training is turning a human being into its exact opposite.

6.  All of the design of the human animal was purpose-
    ful. Some of the necessary components have had
    unfortunate secondary effects.

7.  Fear is an excellent survival mechanism whether
    you are riding a subway or running through a jun-
    gle. It is apparently so necessary to the human psy-
    che that artificial fear is a large industry. Roller
    coasters, horror movies, haunted houses on
    Halloween; humans love to have the shit scared out
    of them.

8.  There was a rumor circulating for quite some time
    in Los Angeles, to the effect that in a nationwide
    comparison of amusement park rides measured
    from one to four, the San Diego Freeway had rated a
    five. It must be assumed that people are willing to
    participate in such madness as 'rush hours' because
    the human animal functions best with daily doses
    of fear.

9.  (We wonder how they would market "Vitamin F"?)
    (Do not be surprised if someone now tries!)

10. Courage is doing that which you would least like to
    do at that moment. Going to work at a job you hate
    can take as much courage as charging an enemy
    machine gun nest. A housewife who feels helplessly
    trapped, and whose only escape is her daily dose of
    electronic fantasy; she should get a medal when she
    summons the courage to turn off her television and
    fix dinner for her family.

11. Do not blame yourself for being afraid. You are built to be that way: so accept it and begin to deal with it. Determine first what it is that has frightened you, and try to assess if it is really a risk to you. If you do perceive it to so be, find out what you can do to deflect that threat. But do not feel guilty about being a fraidy-cat, for you come from a long and honorable line of them.

12. And guilty you will feel. Clearly guilt does not work perfectly, for its purpose in evolution is to keep people from damaging each other excessively. Is it not **obvious to you stupid bastards that we never intended you murder each other in gas chambers?**

13. There is a remote possibility that all the lives so horribly wasted in that conflict will after all have been worth a great deal. People now living are seeing, and living, an evolutionary change as it happens, and we can hope this presages a psychic change, too.

# ∼Chapter 2∼

1.  You know that guilt does not keep humans from killing each other.

2.  Universally arming and training each individual for self defense, however, will eliminate within a generation or two those who initiate violence.

3.  Man is capable of great anger. The strength from anger can allow you to momentarily dominate a larger opponent, or shake a really stubborn piece of fruit from a tree, or make a really stupid woman lie down and behave. It is never acceptable to direct your anger at an inappropriate target, such as your spouse, your dog, or the driver who cut you off on the freeway. Unless it is really dangerous, driving stupidly should not be a capital offense.

4.  At this time anger has little evolutionary value, although it can be helpful to summon your rage if you must deal with an attacker, or the IRS. There are appropriate ways to handle excessive feelings of anger, and control of your temper is a critical component of your responsibility that you be adequately prepared to defend yourself.

5.  You should not feel guilty if you find yourself angry, you should just stop. Back away from the source of the irritation, or deflect it, if at all possible. People can become addicted to the adrenaline and feeling of power that anger brings, but it is best always to try to diffuse a tense situation. Unlike fear, you do not need daily doses of anger; and you are better off without it.

6.  Nothing will infuriate a Humanette more than your refusal to argue with them. Avoid allowing such a person to use you as food to feed their adrenaline craving. If you agree with a person who then switches positions so they can keep working themself up, you may as well end the conversation. They do not understand that human interaction can involve the exchange of ideas. For such a person, others exist only as objects from which to seek emotional gratification of some kind.

7.  Fear and anger and guilt were included in humans so the species could survive, not for the profit of the local god/vernment.

8.  However, these are not what the human was being sculpted to be: these emotions are only some of the tools we have used in the course of the creation process.

9.  This is entirely different from what humans are being shaped to be.

# ∼Chapter 3∼

1. We told you in the beginning that the reason we began creating life on Earth was to find another way to experience love and joy.

2. Believe it or not, folks; but **you are it**.

3. We tell you three times-we tell you three times-we tell you three times: stop killing each other. Stop hurting each other. Stop leaving unwed babies behind and passing stupid laws.

4. Get rid of the vampires that suck out your life. Get rid of people who encourage physical violence against innocent strangers. Get rid of people who first destroy and then steal your money.

5. Get with the program! We want you to be like us! The reason you exist is to find how many ways there are to experience joy, how many kinds of love. You have unlimited capacity for happiness; we challenge you to try to feel too much.

6. You are the best that we have so far accomplished in our search for god-like life. (No, that is not yet really saying much.) Negative emotions are a necessary part of the design, not the purpose.

7.  The human animal is designed **for**, among other things; nobility, courage, and honor. Responsibility for one's own actions is not the highest human virtue, it is the only one.

8.  You are made for joy and love. The more you love yourself the more you will love others, and the more joy there will be for all. The Golden Rule might better suggest that you do unto yourself what you would have others do unto you. It was absolutely correct, when it was so well observed by your Bard, that being true to oneself would mean that one would automatically also be true to others.

9.  Giving yourself the right to live for joy and love will eventually encourage others to do so. There are a great many evil influences in the world, and some do not bode at all well for the future survival of humanity. The sooner each person begins trying to counteract those forces, the better chance you have that we will prevail.

10. You are not doing the will of the gods when you kill another because their beliefs do not meet your approval. You are not doing the will of the gods when you try to cause others to feel fear and guilt for any reason. You are not doing the will of the gods when you require your victims to foot the bill for all that causing and killing.

11. If you ask what man is, the answer at this time may well be, that man is the animal that manipulates.

*Lawyers, Book Two*

# Cannon Fodder Songs

# ～Chapter 4～

1.  Three hundred years ago only fifteen percent of the population could read and write.

2.  Among this year's crop of high school graduates, 85% will be unable to compose a paragraph, punctuate a sentence, or correct simple spelling errors. Forced schooling paid for with money taken forcibly is the government version of 'education,' and the results do not appear to be worth the effort.

3.  Unless "public schools" have another purpose than helping children learn, they are a miserable failure.

4.  Teaching future citizens to be gullible enough to vote, buy, and pay taxes on command, leaps to mind. So does training future soldiers.

5.  Taxpayers can sometimes be dunned eight or nine different ways for the education of others, such as with property and sales taxes, but consider just one example: look at what happens when the government decides to give you a college.

6.    **How To Get A Free Education**

First you pay for consultants to pick the site. Then the land is 'condemned,' which means, "I have a gun and I want your land, and this is how much I will pay you for it. Of course, this is for your good." Then your tax dollars pay for the land.

Then you pay for more consultants to select an 'architect.' These are people who are raised in caves until they are let loose to make life difficult for humans. You also pay the architect.

Do not be confused if the bulldozers and drivers to clear the site, and the materials and the construction workers, are paid for by a "bond issue." This means they are spending money that you will be paying for years to come.

Once the lovely new campus is built, then you get to pay for operating it. The staff will outnumber the instructors two or three to one, and will likely all come from that previously mentioned eighty-five percent. So will most of the instructors.

These instructors are people who are paid very large salaries for comparatively little work. Their main function seems to be reading to a class from a text unfamiliar to the instructor. This may be varied by repeating the material aloud after reading it, or by writing it on the blackboard.

In the case of a doctor or lawyer, the student may then 'borrow' upwards of a hundred thousand dollars from you (by force!), to pay someone to read to them.

7.    This is how you get a free education.

# ∾Chapter 5∾

1. God/vernments love to make everything either forbidden or compulsory. Education is compulsory. Judging from the results, knowledge seems to be forbidden.

2. Many governments make religion or lack thereof mandatory. Humans appear to have a very slippery grasp on what their gods should be, and they seem to change their minds frequently. Strangest of all are those people who insist that their god is the One True God.

3. The same genocidal psychopath has been claimed by at least three major religions, and this mistaken concept has, by itself, been responsible for untold misery. By whatever name, we disown Jehovah; we do not slaughter our children from pique or jealousy, and we do not ever want you to do so either.

4. Many of the people who claim to speak in this villain's name do so not for the profit, but for the power. The way to a man's wallet is through his heart: if you can confuse and torture a person enough—while assuring him it is for his good and

that he deserves the pain—he will do or say whatever you tell him, just to be left alone for a while.

5. The sales pitch seems to go like this: You are evil because you have offended my god, who is very powerful. If you do not do what I claim my god wants, you will suffer horribly. But if you do become one of my disciples, if you give me your money and try to be as unhappy as I; then you get to hope I will tell you to beat up the disciples from the church down the street; and my god will make you rich and powerful someday.

6. Well, people bought the Edsel, too.

7. We do not recommend any of the current Judeo-Christian death cults, including Satanism. Revivals of some of the gods that predominated before Christ and Mohammed will give people a much better chance of finding us, when the search is a gentle and loving one.

8. Though we disapprove rather strongly of some things, the gods do not hate. That is a human invention.

9. We disapprove of hateful actions, of teaching children to hate, and especially of teaching a person they should hate themself.

10. If those who tell you to hate yourself are not speaking for the gods, who might they be speaking to benefit?

*Lawyers, Book Three*

# Do You Hate Your Hair?

# ∼Chapter 6∼

1.  Madison Avenue will go down in history as the creators of emotional pollution.

2.  The picture of itself that humanity receives, from the press, the pulpit, and the schoolteacher's desk, is far from the reality of what man is; and is especially far from what man is capable of being.

3.  Applying toxic salts to your skin, in order to make the pores swell shut and prevent your body's proper function, is called wearing an antiperspirant. There are better ways to smell better, such as bathing often and wearing clean clothes; and eating good fresh things will help make your scent good and fresh.

4.  Adaptability is a prime survival characteristic in humans, and imitation is one facet of that. It is not surprising that when one primate discovers how to do something interesting with their hair, other primates will try to do the same. Some will be frustrated and unhappy because they cannot accomplish it.

5.  No one can be sure whether their hair should be short or long, straight or curly, stiff with spray or

flying in the breeze, or what color it should be. The only thing the marketers appear to agree on, is that you need to be different from the way you were designed to look and feel.

6.  Preparations to change the smell and texture of your skin; stuff by the truckload to overcome the horrors of what shoes do to your feet. Several sorts of things for your genitals and dozens of products for your mouth. All of these products contain elements toxic to the human system. Why do you buy them?

7.  The more you alter your body chemistry, the more you will need to continue to alter it. In case you are still unsure, bathing and cleanliness are not sins; if anything, it is filth that is sinful. The practice of using scent to hide unpleasant body odor comes to you from cultures where the fun of splashing in water and the joy of being clean are not allowed.

8.  Humans emit an 'odorless odor' designed to signal availability for mating. You cannot cover your natural pheromone with perfume or cologne; nor can you enhance it.

9.  It is better to increase your desirability as a mate by developing your own assets than by advertising that which you do not have. Spending money for a health spa may get you into shape; but the same money invested in martial arts training will not only get you in better shape, it will leave you speaking softly and walking tall.

10. A man will appeal more to women if he is able to protect them. And men are designed to prefer women who do not appear overly dependent; that is, women who can take care of themselves.

11. Simply accepting yourself with a gentle understanding may be the most powerful aphrodisiac possible. Improving your life in any way, such as going to school or getting into shape, will bring multiple benefits. As your consciousness moves toward harmony with yourself, it will be reflected in your desire to feel good about yourself.

12. There are two likely reactions when you see a happy person. When you meet someone who clearly likes themself and enjoys life, do you hate and envy them? Or do you like them, and want to be like them? Obviously if you cannot tolerate joy in another, you will not have much of it for yourself.

13. If you do wish to have a life of joy and love, it will at once be clear to you that the way to **get** more of these things is to **give** them. When a stranger snarls at you, offer them sympathy; for obviously not only are they having a bad day or a bad life, but you have an advantage in at least knowing happiness is possible.

14. Those who profit financially or emotionally from increasing your unhappiness have so managed to insinuate their poison into every facet of your life, there is no chance you will ever enjoy that life unless you begin at once to arm yourself: physically, morally, and with all the knowledge you can acquire.

15. It is difficult to choose among such things as war, religion, and censorship when you are seeking to warn of the worst things humans do to each other. But there is one particular insanity that merits a bit more discussion.

16. Forget about the Bandersnatch, kids: beware of the Justice Industry.

# ∼Chapter 7∼

1. 'The Law' is a strong contender for the award for the Worst Oppressive Agency.

2. When people demand you respect 'the law,' do they expect you to stand up and salute National Frozen Food Week? Should you look up to some beer-guzzling bribe-taking slob simply because he has a badge and a gun?

3. America is not a country of laws. It is a country of **lawyers**.

4. The Seven Hundred Thousand Club is the second most exclusive fraternity in the world. We almost admire the ABA: an attorney is such an amazing creation. Lawyers are responsible, by making it workable for the police to act as they do, for a great part of what the Justice Industry is today.

5. Now the same 'criminals' who brought tea to the American colonists, and rum to the Great Gatsbys, account for most of the activity and income of the justice industry by importing "dope."

6.  (It is a shame people did not try harder instead to keep prohibition in force. Alcohol is much worse for people than are most recreational drugs.)

7.  The judges, police and prosecutors that are so busy filling your expensive prisons with non-violent offenders can only have one possible motivation. They want the violent criminals out on your streets committing crimes.

8.  An officer who chooses to use his limited time persecuting innocent entrepreneurs instead of investigating a real crime; the prosecutor who offers a plea bargain, not because anyone has been harmed, but because he has a cheap conviction to better his record; the judge that chooses to sentence to prison a person who has committed not a crime, but a violation that is more on the level of over-parking at a meter: each of these professional dispensers of 'justice' makes a decision that what a person does privately to themselves is a greater risk to society than what is done violently to innocent strangers.

9.  We disagree.

10. Extorting huge sums of money from citizens at gunpoint, to finance enforcement of laws against such things as your choices in sexual positions, on the pretext that the good of society requires such interference: this is the reality of the justice industry.

11. Judging from their actions, the industry exists not to keep you from suffering the effects of crime, but to control your personal life.

12. To get a law passed, you need; a big mouth, ability to rally other bigmouths, and an elected official who wants publicity (!). The Law is mainly a collection of the prejudices of those who hate their own lives and most especially want to destroy the joy in life for all others.

13. If you think it is wrong for a woman to abort an unwanted child, there is a very simple solution. Offer to adopt the baby and pay for the mother's care. No one is 'pro-abortion;' no woman has **ever** told a friend with glee, "Guess what! I'm pregnant! Now I get to have an abortion!"

14. You do not have the right to murder people for choosing to earn a living at a woman's health clinic. If you want to prevent abortions, you may not terrorize or harass those who have not interfered with you. Your appointment as the avenging angel is hereby withdrawn. So KYFHO.

15. It does not make you moral to slaughter someone else for holding a belief with which you disagree.

# ~Chapter 8~

1.  Obviously we cannot keep you from doing such evil and stupid things, to yourselves and to each other.

2.  But please stop blaming it on the gods!

3.  It does not even say in the Judeo-Christian Bible that Thou Shalt Not smoke marijuana. Perhaps this is because the use of that particular substance was so endemic in the culture of the authors, it never occurred to them not to use it. Or even to forbid it for others.

4.  The godfearing churchgoing citizen, puffing on his cigarette and condemning those who smoke another kind of cigarette, does not hate the other smoker because his god has commanded him to so hate. He wants to punish the other smoker for breaking a rule. He wants to punish anyone who might have a good time.

5.  A small group of crackpots can make a big enough noise to get the attention of any legislator with nothing better to do, or who can find time for the crackpots in between Frozen Food Week and Dental

Health Month. These lice in the pubic hair of society are in agreement in only their hysterical hatred of any semblance of human pleasure.

6.  These people use the power of the state, which is the power of life and death, to force others to obey their own standards of behavior. Pay attention here: you are not-not-**not** allowed to kill someone because they dare to enjoy life more than you.

7.  Long version: "I have been told all my life to hate and fear pleasure. If you experience pleasure by doing what is 'wrong,' then what I have been told all my life is a lie; and I can not face the fact that I have lived my whole life believing lies. As you and I cannot co-exist in the world I have been taught to believe in, one of us cannot continue to exist. My rules say **you** are wrong, and I will try to crush or kill you if I can, because I have to continue living."

8.  Short version: "There ought to be a law."

9.  This is why you suffer from the wish to keep others from experiencing pleasure, and that is what that wish really means.

10. Wake up, folks. You have been lied to, laughed at, manipulated and cheated by every institution that you trust.

11. It is not natural for you to hate and envy one who has managed to loosen his own shackles the tiniest bit. Instead you should turn your anger on those who have so badly screwed up your life. You should hate those who enslave you, if you must hate some-

one. Do not take it out on your fellow slave, who is only trying to make himself free.

12. Turn your enmity toward those who deserve it: hate those who have hurt you so dreadfully for their own profit.

# ∽Chapter 9∽

1.  If you have been harboring a suspicion that you are nothing but a patsy, a sheep, and a source of income, there is hope for you.

2.  You have a better chance at stopping the destruction of your life if you know who is doing it to you, and how, and why.

3.  A doctor profits when you are sick. A cop is happy when you are victimized. The job of your priest is to destroy your self worth.

4.  Your first job as a 'good citizen' is to be a sick, stupid, groveling victim. Your second job is to pay and pay and pay and pay for a promise of relieving those conditions. The promise is all you ever get: your money will never buy you relief from your torturers.

5.  Giving money to them only encourages them. The billions of dollars spent in the War Against Peaceful Citizens Who Choose to Use Recreational Drugs has only whetted their appetite to control you. The only effect that the "War on Drugs" can have on your life if you do not choose to use, is that there are

vicious criminals on your streets because your prisons are filled with non-violent offenders.

6.  Judge their intentions by their actions. The agents of the justice industry want you to suffer from violent crime.

7.  You know your government lies to you. When they tell you it is for your good that you suffer horrible penalties should you dare try to find a means of escape, and that your duty is to hate and envy those who do seek release; should you not doubt what they say?

8.  If someone else's pleasure causes you pain, you do not have the right to have them put to death. This is the unstated promise every god/vernment offers to you in return for your willingness to suffer on command, and the justice industry is the tool they flourish as a means of keeping that promise.

9.  You are created to be happy. Whatever you wish to eat, drink, smoke, or consensually sleep with is good for you, as long as it causes no harm to others. If it causes someone else to suffer when you enjoy life, that is their problem.

# ∽Chapter 10∽

1.  When citizens can defend themselves, the justice industry will be obsolete.

2.  **They Will Not Tell You The Truth.**

3.  They will not tell you the real reason laws against pleasure are so vigorously enforced. They will **not** tell you the real reason they want you unarmed and helpless.

4.  There will always be a forum needed where citizens can adjudicate the balancing of rights and responsibilities in society. Human society does not need rulers who punish people for innocent pleasure.

5.  You do not need to be told you are worthless. You do not need to be manipulated emotionally. You do not need to be taxed, literally, to death.

6.  You do need to understand what you are, and be that. You need to understand that you have more than just a right to enjoy your life: you have an obligation.

7.  You need to know the truth. Do not accept **anything** your god/vernment says! Check it against logic,

against common sense; and above all, check it against the facts. Bill Clinton's fictitious "balanced budget" exists only because of one magic phrase. (Ever hear the words *"off budget,"* Mr. President? Some people have....)

8. You do not need multi-billion dollar industries making private choices for you. You do not need to pay those billions out to those who wish to punish you for trying to be happy.

9. You need to educate yourself, believe in your own goodness, and trust your ability to make correct 'moral' choices. It is moral to enjoy your own life. It is **very** wrong to try to keep others from enjoying their life.

10. And if you try to initiate violence against another, you ~~probably~~ need to be killed.

# Last Concatenation:
## Sex? Again?

# ~Psongs, Book Four~

# Colpo di Fulmine

# ∾Chapter 1∾

1.  We herewith apologize to Heloise and Abelard, and to all those who may have suffered from that peculiar affliction.

2.  We refer, of course, to love at first sight.

3.  A significant portion of humanity has inherited a vestige of what human scientists will tell you is called 'the pair-bonding response.' Unfortunately all of the distress that this phenomenon has caused through the years has been to no avail.

4.  Before we resorted to the tragic extreme of introducing violence, every alternative solution to the sexual crisis was tested. Increasing sexual desire and pleasure did not serve to induce humans to mate in the face of increasing difficulty, so the obvious next step was to heighten the 'emotional' attraction. At least it seemed like a good idea at the time.

5.  The response was not fully developed when we abandoned the effort, for it became clear it was not going to work. Therefore the mechanism is faulty

and imperfect; and because it has no survival value, it is no longer universal.

6. Obviously, creating a lifelong emotional bond between two people does not remove physical barriers to copulation. Taken far enough, it would become a detriment to survival; for when emotional and physical attraction did not suffice and violence became necessary, being unable to harm the woman would dampen lust.

7. Another reason it does not work is the complexity of humans. Swans need not hold similar political beliefs nor have compatible careers, and they are programmed to agree on methods for raising goslings. It is not quite so simple for mankind.

8. And causing two people to mate only with each other is a terrific hindrance to the genetic variety we try so hard to create.

9. Every culture has a word or phrase for that incredible moment when two complete strangers become instantly and irrevocably linked, but so far no one seems to have discovered the true explanation.

10. It will not happen to everyone, and you will not know ahead of time if you carry the gene for pair-bonding. In fact you will probably not realize until long after the event that you may be a victim.

11. If you carry the gene, sometime near the end of puberty you will become receptive. You will be triggered the first time you come within smelling distance (pheromone range) of someone of the opposite

sex who is also receptive. Voila! You are in love: instantly, passionately, and permanently. If you have grown up in a small town or an isolated area, this can happen at any time in life, not just in puberty.

12. Many young romantics will hear of this and leap to the conclusion that this week's pimple prince is her one true love. Please do not. We are specifically not talking about infatuation, which can be intense but is never long lasting. Time is the only way to be sure you are not a victim. Give yourself a minimum of five years, and preferably at least ten: if after that time the intensity has not diminished (and particularly if it has increased), you can probably assume the feeling will not go away any time soon.

# ∼Chapter 2∼

1. The average garden snail has a better and more rewarding sex life than the average human.

2. The snail in question has a full set of both male and female organs for reproduction, and both sets are simultaneously engaged in the course of intercourse; and then both snails tip their hats, and go their respective merry ways.

3. The bonding process is also workable for less complex animals than man, but even an irresistible sexual and emotional attraction was not enough to keep man breeding. However, as it does not **preclude** its victim's ability to mate, there was never a reason to remove it. Yes, the gods make mistakes and leave you to clean up the mess. Live with it.

4. Falling hopelessly in love with a person from another race, religion, or socio-economic class will make the lovers crazy every time. The object of desire may be totally inappropriate, but this kind of 'love' does not depend on respect or trust or compatibility; and many victims try desperately to reject or deny the compulsion.

5. Nowadays such a passion usually causes more grief than pleasure to the sufferers. Success in rejecting the object of desire always leaves both parties feeling like an animal that has gnawed off a leg to escape a trap; for they have bought freedom only by leaving a part of themselves behind.

6. Humans can be extremely contrary; and being told even by one's own body and soul, that you must love this person and no other, often causes a bonded mate to become the last person on earth the bonded one wants to mate with.

7. Everyone knows of couples who marry and divorce and marry again: people who can live neither with nor without each other. If you do not know of a living example from the news and gossip columns, there are plenty of examples in your literature; and it might be fun to guess who they are. Cathy and Heathcliff? Romeo and Juliet? Was this Leila's dilemma?

8. Many humans marry and remain faithful for life, and we might be concerned about the efficacy of societal training if we knew not the cause. But the call from the god/vernments for monogamy finds many receptive ears; because although man was first designed to seek variety, he was partially redesigned for exclusivity. Each man and woman spends their entire life on a tightrope: leaning now toward one special one; later toward another, any other.

9. There is no easy, pop-psychology solution for humans. The bottom line is that you will spend your life being torn in two directions, and you can

find great unhappiness by trying to believe you are meant only for one or the other.

10. One phenomenon that puzzles many is why a battered woman continues to forgive and continues to allow the battering. There is a small element of mutual attraction in such a relationship, but they can be largely accounted for by a genetic heritage that makes men violent and women tolerant of it.

# ∼Chapter 3∼

1. Sex is the only game in town; and if it feels as if you can't win for losing, you are probably playing it exactly right.

2. If you wish more from your relationships than progeny, you must begin avoiding disappointment by not setting your expectations unrealistically.

3. No one can choose 'love at first sight' for themselves (you would not want to if you could) but you already know that not even the gods can make a man stay when he is ready to go.

4. If you are a man, expect rejection. There just are not enough women to go around, and by definition there could never be. Women will continue to be selective. Give some thought to keeping the woman who has already said yes, and smile at those who say no.

5. If you are a woman, realize that every man arrives in your life with a round trip ticket in his hand. You can enjoy the moment best if you accept that it will end; and you can enjoy **him** a lot more if you love

him for what he is, instead of hurting yourself over what he is not.

6. Women desire and enjoy sex **at least** as much as men, and men need love all the more because it is often so very difficult for them to ask for it. Do not make the mistake of forcing your partner to limit how much they can enjoy you, by trying to force either of you into a preconceived mold that will never fit.

7. Sex is going to be around for a long time; and it won't get any better unless you improve it for yourself.

8. And there is really only one way to do that.

# ~Chapter 4~

1.  If you feel you need someone special in your life, buy a dog.

2.  If 'need' is all you have to offer, why should anyone have anything to offer you?

3.  The more you have to offer to yourself, the more you have to offer to your prospective partner. We do not intend this to be saccharine advice like "get a hobby," although that in itself is not a bad idea. What we mean is that you must reach inward for fulfillment, instead of trying to find an outside source for filling the holes.

4.  The holes in your soul come from loss of contact with the gods. This is the emptiness that people feel and try frantically to fill; with buying and killing, and by sleeping with anything that moves. Seek the gods within you and you are guaranteed true love.

5.  Like in real estate, the three most important things in a relationship are: communication, communication, and communication.

6.  A pet is indeed excellent training; both in dealing with the emotional needs of another being, and in

learning to communicate with another soul. You will be well off to assume that in dealing with a human, you are trying to mate with a visitor from another planet, rather than trying to make a connection with someone like yourself.

7.  The only similarities are pain, fear, and a desire for love. Men and women do not even achieve sexual satisfaction from the same activity.

8.  Men still get off in the tried and true way, but the movement of the female vagina also removed the female sexual reward. It was faster and easier for the gods, when the male began going at her from the wrong direction, to try to make the clitoris accessible another way. Otherwise we would have had to move the blasted thing around to the opposite side of the vagina: it was easier to just push it straight through the skin.

9.  Note: if you have been watching the scorecard, you are aware that this last-minute alteration of the female anatomy came **after** the introduction of violence. The physical ability to procreate was not enough. Female pleasure was and is required for evolutionary success.

10.  It helps a lot toward success in a relationship, too. Sex manuals abound and you can find all the instruction you desire; the single critical element is a genuine commitment to your partner's pleasure. A good lover need not worry about money or looks or skill on the dance floor. Body cleanliness, patience, and a desire for learning how to please will rate you far higher.

11. Such an attitude in bed will be reflected in your walk and talk when you are out of bed, and you will draw lovers by the score.

12. Sex comes in a neat, workable package for every other species, but humans are no longer designed so that the female achieves orgasm from the procreative act.

13. We have gone to great effort to preserve this function; please use it. The male partner should always see to the satisfaction of the female before he seeks his own. Women very rarely can achieve orgasm from only penile stimulation: **they are no longer designed for it.**

14. The famous "G-spot" is actually the leftover nerve bundle where the clitoris used to be when the male always mounted from the rear, and stimulation of that spot can occasionally satisfy a woman who is sufficiently aroused.

15. But the clitoris was designed as the center of action, and the fact that it has moved simply changes the action a bit.

16. The male on his back with the female astride is very workable for both, and the woman may have a good chance to reach satisfaction. Having the firm support of a penis behind it makes the clitoris more accessible and more sensitive, and stimulation of it from both sides at once can far more than double her pleasure.

17. But the way to get unlimited pleasure is an all out attempt to give it.

# ∼Chapter 5∼

1.  People are not snails. Snails are not cursed with such an entertaining sex life.

2.  People have suffered throughout history, in numbers large and small, because your sex life is so screwed up. Since you are now so remarkably successful at procreation anyway, there is no reason for us to try to make it better. But you can make it better for yourself.

3.  Those who shriek with outrage about 'sex education' will be even more against teaching children how to **enjoy** sex. They do not want to protect children; they want to prevent, in a word, life. Ignore them.

4.  Then teach children **right**. Teach them the basics of biology and reproduction. Tell them about disease and responsibility. And let them learn the real truth: that the human body is designed to seek and to give the maximum possible pleasure.

5.  Do not teach them to lie about sex, and do not teach them fear and shame. Love of pleasure is natural. It should be put into a context of correct time and

place, not rejected and suppressed. Teach a child that giving themself pleasure is a very human function.

6.  (Your genitals are within reach of your hands. It would seem obvious that we mean you to be able to reach them.)

7.  Humans are designed to seek pleasure with every erg of energy they do not need for survival. Joy is the reason humans exist, and to deny that urge is a guarantee of physical, emotional, and social sickness.

8.  You have the best chance of winning the game of love when you go into it knowing you are going to lose. Most women are going to reject you: most men are going to leave you.

9.  Certainly paint and perfume yourself all you like; dress in your best and flirt till you fall. Enjoy the opposite sex as much as you can—you are both designed for it—enjoy them for what they are, instead of what you wish they would be.

10. Expect courtesy, cleanliness and generosity; expect as much respect as you are entitled to; demand the minimum of attention needed for mutual satisfaction.

11. Just do not expect to live happily ever after. It can happen; but the odds are that if you **are** happy, it will not be together.

12. We bailed you out of the worst scrape a species has ever survived, and though there are some unfortunate side effects, you are much improved for the experience.

13. We are doing all this one step at a time, correcting problems as they appear; and not every choice has turned out to be the best one. C'est la vie.

14. You can curse us for having made errors that make your life so difficult. Or you can do the best you can with what you've got. The choice is yours; continue to suffer, or just bear it and keep grinning.

# Final Testament:
# A Lever and a Place to Stand

~Book Thirteen~

# Shtark Zich

# ⮱Chapter 1⮰

1. Listen, dear children, and you shall hear, how your liberation may soon be near.

2. You are not our laboratory rats. **You are us.**

3. You are the expression of the gods of the existence of love and joy. You are our means of reaching for life.

4. Doing the will of the gods means being the best human you can be. It means we want you to be happy, joyous, and free.

5. Knowledge is power, wealth, and happiness. Learning is far more addictive a drug than any chemical man has devised. The key to understanding yourself is educating yourself.

6. You have been screwed from the start. Your **only** choice is whether to help screw yourself or to fight back.

7. You are entitled to a peaceful life, free of forceful intervention from others. You are entitled to use as much force as necessary to keep anyone from interfering violently with your peaceful pursuits.

8.  The decision to go armed carries tremendous respon-
    sibility. Above all you must control your temper.
    Absolute control of your emotions is at all times
    mandatory. There is simply no excuse, never has been
    and never will be an excuse, **there can be no justifica-
    tion,** for using violence against a person who has not
    threatened you with physical harm.

9.  There are many people who want to kill you for not
    doing as they say. If you can still possibly doubt
    that, there are many new career opportunities avail-
    able in most abortion clinics. People have been
    taught by government and by "god" that it is moral
    to kill: for what amounts to any reason, or no rea-
    son at all.

10. There are several available defenses against those
    who plot and preach your destruction.

11. Those who try to teach you to hate your hair, your
    facial features, and your natural body scents; who
    tell you that you should be ashamed of the car you
    drive or the home you live in; who are, in fact,
    telling you that you should hate your own life; are
    they of value to your life? Or should you, perhaps,
    just ignore them?

12. Do you need to pay armed wolf-packs to roam
    your streets, slavering to pounce on anyone who
    might have some fun? Do you need a justice indus-
    try that mainly exists to control your sex life and
    your recreation?

13. The human body is not obscene, and we despise those of you who despise our best work. Why do you pay people to tell you to hate that which we so clearly love?

14. We reject obscenity, profanity, sacrilege and heresy. Such filth is remanded to the minds capable of such self-hatred. We recommend that you most strenuously request a refund from those that have lied to you about the true nature of the gods.

15. Do you need a god, or a government, to lie to you and terrorize you, for your own good?

# ⧼Chapter 2⧽

1. The Mafia would surely run the government better than the hoodlums you people elect.

2. 'The Family' is as least a good enough businessman to realize there is far more profit from encouraging 'vice' than there is in preventing it.

3. When you select for your highest office a man who has not only broken his most sacred vow but has a lifelong habit of weaseling when it matters, do not be surprised that he also lacks the balls to be a good businessman.

4. (For heaven's sake, this man was **struck dumb** during his election campaign! What do you people need, **skywriting**?)

5. Giving up so much of your humanity to the control of others also means losing your adaptability. Many people would rather die, or see you die, before they admit being lifelong suckers. These people will not have much chance to achieve freedom.

6. The "Contract with America" is laughably typical of the absolute blind arrogance with which your rulers

view you. It would appear that most of the signatories to that "contract" are unaware of haven taken any part in the negotiations.

7. You have a very limited span on Earth. If we had intended you spend it as nothing more than a cog in the state's machine, we would simply have created a set of tinker toys.

8. We do not expect each person to reach their own full potential. We only expect you to try. But the way the system is rigged now, almost no one has a chance to be as happy as they might be.

9. The Pope did not call the President to discuss how to keep you in a helpless, docile state. He did not have to. They both have the same goals.

10. The plot is to maximize your fear and confusion and hopelessness. It is not one great universal plan; rather it is the aggregate of the manipulations of every person who hates life and strives to keep others from enjoying it.

11. We would like to see each of our creations reaching for life and love and joy as they are supposed to do. Structure your life for pleasure; budget the luxuries first. And above all, be prepared to defend your right to so live.

# ∾Chapter 3∾

1. We never foresaw Dachau when we created the human race.

2. We might have had second thoughts.

3. To destroy a people, first you disarm them. When you willingly disarm yourself, you are voluntarily taking the first step toward your own destruction.

4. A six-gun on your hip will discourage most muggers and some tax collectors (pardon the redundancy), though even that may not suffice to keep you clear of orange robes at airports.

5. We cannot emphasize enough that we do not-Not-NOT want you to go out and buy a gun and strap it on! Do you understand?

6. You must acquire training before you decide to go armed, and we most strongly recommend learning unarmed self defense first.

7. You must also arm yourself morally and mentally. The decision to go armed is a proclamation of social responsibility.

8.   There is a deep hunger in every person for commun-
     ion with the gods. The place to seek the gods is within:
     and the way you begin the search is by turning your
     back on all those who would keep you in chains.

9.   Listen to your heart, your conscience, and your
     hunches; these are all names you have given to the
     best within you trying to get out. The more you are
     willing to listen to the voices of the gods within you
     telling you the truth, the easier it will be for you to
     hear when others speak falsely.

10.  Arm yourself mentally against your controllers by
     educating yourself. Begin at once and never stop.
     Check the facts always, and compare the opinions of
     others against their own ignorance and prejudices.
     Make sure your own conclusions are based on facts
     rather than emotions.

11.  Defend yourself morally by always doing what you
     know is right, no matter how painful it may be at
     the moment. If another tries to tell you something
     is right or wrong, find out upon what facts their
     opinion is based and form your own opinion. A
     moral decision can **never** be made for you: the
     responsibility for your choices must rest on your
     shoulders and yours alone, always.

12.  Defend yourself physically against the vermin who
     would threaten you or yours. Never initiate vio-
     lence; always respond when another does. Use as
     much force as you need to stop such violence, and
     to ensure that it can not happen again.

13. You owe it to yourself to go armed; and to your children and your community and your planet. Preventing violence is the responsibility of every person on Earth.

14. Then mind your own business, and live your own good life.

·

## Book Fourteen

# It Says it in the Bible

# #A—How to be Human

The likelihood that you are right increases in direct proportion to the number of people trying to convince you that you are wrong.

The gods wanted to save humans from extinction: the use of violence was a desperate last resort. That is also the only reason you should ever resort to force. Walking away is best when it is possible: when it is not, you must be prepared to defend yourself.

Educate yourself, love yourself, liberate yourself. No one can do any of these things for you: you must always do the important things in life for yourself.

A parking place, a rainbow, a penny on the street: these are gifts from the gods. Enjoy them.

Teach your children to love themselves, each other and their world; then they will also love you. Teach yourself the same things, and you will love every part of your life.

If nice guys finish last, does that mean they live the longest?

# #B—The Environment

Clean up the Oglalla Reservoir before you make the entire center of the country uninhabitable.

No one has the right to foul the air and waters. Stop it at once.

For example: the suggestion that one who wishes to discharge into a river being required to place their water intake directly downstream from their outlet, is one that can be adapted to cover most sources of pollution.

This applies equally to industry and to automobiles. Cars are one of the nuttier things humans do anyway; and the danger of putting a person who has trouble with shoe-tying inside a ton of self-propelled death is matched by the destructiveness of their exhaust. These folks need to pay the full cost of their pleasures.

No other animal fouls its own nest to the extent that man does. Tossing a can or a butt on the ground is an act of hatred toward your own life and the lives others, and toward the sweet earth that nourishes you all. This is **our** Earth: leave it or leave it alone.

# #C—Death and Taxes

Every living thing will someday die. Death is inevitable. Taxes are not.

That so many people equate extortion and theft with the natural processes of life is evidence of how completely your rulers own your mind.

The human being is designed to die. He is most decidedly **not** designed to pay taxes.

# #D—Your Body

Go naked early and often. Keeping clean, eating right and staying fit are big boosts to your spiritual well being.

Do not pollute your body with medications. The cure for a headache is almost always food and rest; for a cold it is rest and liquids. Pain is intended as a signal of bodily malfunction. Do not suppress the symptoms, treat the condition that caused the pain.

Try to stay as internally harmonious as possible by avoiding chemicals and denatured foods. Canned and preserved foods not only have little nutritive value, eating them is actually a detriment because they are so difficult to digest.

Likewise your skin is finely tuned to work best in its natural state. Try to keep it free of dirt, clothing and chemicals, and avoid harsh soaps.

You would not dunk a Swiss watch into alcohol, or pour syrup into a Porsche. Your body is a far more intricate piece of machinery: treat it as such.

It is also a more beautiful work of art than any other that man can produce.

# #E—Marriage

If the bad news is that half of all marriages today will end in divorce, does that mean the good news is that the other half will end in death?

You would not bet your life, and the lives of your children, on a coin toss. But that is exactly what you are doing when you go into marriage without forethought.

A limited-duration contract, with peaceful dissolution written in, must obviously take a place in society alongside the till-death-do-us-part kind of marriage.

A contract that provides for division of assets and the care of children is essentially a pre-approved divorce. The addition of an option for renewal would make such an arrangement workable for all except lawyers.

Humans are not designed for lifelong monogamy. A lot of heartbreak will be avoided when humans try to be what they are, instead of trying to be the garbage their god/vernment wants them to be.

# #F—Smoking

The government takes your money to prosecute and imprison those who smoke one kind of leaf, and takes more money to give to those who grow and sell another kind of leaf.

Meanwhile the government uses still more of your money to pay the salary of the Surgeon General, who advises people to smoke the illegal leaf in preference to the one you are subsidizing.

It is appropriate for you to object to someone smoking any substance in an area in which you are enclosed. What a person chooses to smoke in privacy can't **possibly** be any of your business.

It is entirely inappropriate for those who have sworn to protect you to point a gun at you and demand money; and to then turn that money over to their buddies, to grow and market to you **the most poisonous and addictive substance on Earth.**

The leaf the U. S. government spends your money to promote kills at least half a million Americans per year.

But even the least honest government researchers can find, in five thousand years of records, **not one death** from smoking marijuana. This leaf is also, at about *100* times the price of the subsidized leaf, now the number one cash crop in America.

Supporting one leaf and prohibiting the other is for your own good, of course.

# #G—Sasquatch

There is a group of people organized for the purpose of proving Bigfoot exists, so that they can get laws passed for the protection of the species. (No kidding, there really is.)

It strikes us that these creatures are at least as well protected by disbelief in their existence as they could be by the Federal Government.

If you want a solution to Earth's racial problems, why not just for the hell of it try persuasion instead of coercion?

We created separate strains of humanity so that they could be re-blended and further perfected. Each strain has desirable characteristics, and we love each equally.

Put interracial families in all of your stories and advertising; and within a generation, racism on Earth may only be a horrible memory.

None of the gods is black or white or brown or yellow, or pink or purple or green: we are all mongrels and half-breeds. And we are the best.

# #H—Sales Tax

Every person needs permission from the government to transact private business, and in some places the local rulers extort as much as ten percent of the value of the transaction for granting that permission.

Two individuals may not conduct business without first bribing those who would imprison or kill them should the individuals try to keep their private affairs private.

Nobody gives a damn what the Emperor wears, but you pay for his imaginary clothing with very real money.

# #I—The World's Greatest Lover

Every organism has two drives: to survive and to reproduce. Every choice that each being makes will be in furtherance of one or the other of those two imperatives.

Humans need spend comparatively little energy choosing for survival. Therefore nearly every choice a human makes will be directed by their sex drive.

You should be worried only if you **don't** think about sex nearly all the time, in one form or another.

The only thing needed to be a good lover is to learn, learn, learn. Learn at least a minimum about body chemistry and reproductive biology. Learn what makes each separate inch of your lover's body feel best.

Learn what hurts you, and why. Learn what hurts others, and try to not.

When you love yourself from deep within, you will be everyone's beloved. Care about yourself and care about your partners, and we will guarantee you great sex.

# #J—Capital Punishment

State-imposed death penalty laws act as an encouragement to crime, not as a deterrent.

There are three kinds of crimes that generally are considered extreme enough by society to rate the ultimate sanction.

The first can be disposed of quickly: putting a two-bit hood to death for a stickup gone wrong will not stop other holdups. These peabrains do not tend to take such remote contingencies into account.

The other two have the same appeal for the killer, as either is likely to outrage society enough to provoke the desired reaction. Capital punishment is usually reserved as a reward for killing enough people in a brutal enough fashion; or for killing a famous or powerful person, such as a policeman or a politician.

Such a killing is the result of a decision that the victim must die so that the killer may, in some fashion, continue to live.

If you learn only one thing from reading these words, it is most important that you learn to understand the mind of such a killer.

Try to imagine the emptiness of a soul that looks forward to a life on death row, as **the best that they can hope for.**

The ~~man~~ scratch that; the creature that killed John Lennon acquired a life and an identity. For the rest of his life he was known as the one that killed John Lennon.

Do not reward such people by promising them the obliteration they crave. Their hatred of themselves should not be the cause of your life's ending. If a person finds no value in their own life, he may try to find a value by killing an innocent person. Society should not offer to relieve them of responsibility for their own life.

Making it an alternative, to quietly and painlessly check out when desired, will drastically reduce the number of people who kill because they wish to die.

# #K—Fireworks

There is a growing trend in the United States which deserves a special mention.

Please beware of people who advocate only public celebrations of the Fourth of July.

The arguments against private celebrations are reasonable—no one wants children maimed or property damaged—but these arguments are entirely missing the point!

Setting off fireworks in your driveway is a symbol for the personal risk each person chose to take in order to be free. It is essential to maintain this tradition, and to keep sacred this last celebration of individual freedom.

Communist governments are enormously fond of holding mass political meetings to glorify their ownership of the people. Gathering in an arena to watch pretty lights is hardly symbolic of the spirit of liberty that caused the Founding Fathers to risk their "fortunes, lives, and sacred honor."

Do not allow your government to trick you out of your last real American right. Too many people paid the ultimate price for you to have it.

# #L—Sin

The Devil is of course an invention of man. The gods do indeed wish to tempt you to pleasure, but we certainly do not intend to punish those who accept our sweet invitation.

Those who hate life call any form of enjoyment evil. But look at their motive.

It is as simple as denying others what they themselves cannot enjoy. Anyone who will tell you that pleasure is wrong is a killer at heart: to hate the enjoyment of life is to hate life itself.

Anyone who hates your 'sin' actually hates **you**, and wishes to punish you for your enjoyment.

Your purpose on Earth is to 'sin.' Enjoy it.

# #M—You Bet Your Life

Were a working man or woman to be allowed to purchase for themself private unemployment or unplanned pregnancy insurance, they would receive far more for their money than they now can from the 'government.'

The current movement on the part of some of your rulers toward forcing everyone to purchase health insurance is but a foot in the door. Why not mandatory life insurance?

That would be the perfect irony, of course: "You will give us your money to buy you life insurance or we will kill you."

Because **every** tax is collected ultimately at the point of a gun. Calling the tax system 'voluntary' is on a par with the other truths your government tells you.

Forcing every working person to pay for the consequences of the unwise few is to point a gun at each taxpayer and say, "You must give up your money because others have a need to be lazy and irresponsible, and you must pay for all needs of all others."

Each hour that you work is an investment in the future. Each dollar you earn, that is taken forcibly from you, is an hour spent in involuntary slavery: working for the benefit of others against your will.

Humanity came into existence without the benefit of government programs. How much more evidence do you need that you will also be better off without those programs now?

# #N—Teach Your Children Well

If you wish to guarantee that your children will grow into dysfunctional adults, teach them that children do not matter.

Once you have laid a good foundation by handling the infant as an inanimate object, you only really need one other technique. Tell them that they have to be adults before they count.

The most charming method is to tell the child that the pleasures of adults are not for them. Tell them that they can not be a valid human being until they grow up, and they will be in a hurry to do that growing.

Tell them that all the good things in life are also reserved for adults. Then watch them try to become adults by embracing those good things.

Such things as liquor and sex are the symbols of adulthood. Children who are taught that they have no worth as children will try to become adults, often by reaching for those symbols.

Parents always decry 'peer pressure' for leading their children astray. But children who are emotionally damaged get that way first from **parent pressure**.

# #O—Entitlements

One of the most preposterous notions humans have spawned is that the world owes anyone a living.

It does, and you are welcome to sleep in any unoccupied cave you can find. Eat all you want of food that no one has cultivated: go ahead! Pick it off the trees!

The world may owe you a living. Your fellow man does not.

# P—Politics

A 'demonstration' is a group of people holding their breaths until they turn blue; they may deserve humor, but not respect. Stopping traffic and such is more serious. By daring you to react, they are using their vulnerability as a weapon against you; and to hell with that. You may have the right to lie down in front of a moving car, but the driver has the right to give you exactly that for which you are asking.

'Elections' are just as silly: an organized way to allow a minority to forcefully impose their will on all those who voted otherwise, and upon all those who did not vote. "My Congressman can beat up your Congressman" is not the only way you could pick your parasites.

The average American will work more than five months out of each year—spend almost half of his waking life, year after year—to pay what he 'owes' to his fellow citizens. Your government will spend that amount in one second.

One half your life disposed of in one second.

Are you really that fucking worthless?

# In the Beginning

# ~Chapter 1~

1.  You have **the right** to feel good about yourself and your life.

2.  You have **the right** to forcibly keep anyone else from interfering with the peaceful enjoyment of that life.

3.  You have a responsibility to yourself and your community to vigorously defend your rights.

4.  Remember that the current working model of a human being is the result of a sexual crisis.

5.  The solution to that crisis allowed humanity to survive, but at the cost of accepting built-in weaknesses.

6.  All of man's unhappiness comes from those weaknesses, and from those who prey upon that vulnerability.

7.  Most of man's major institutions are designed to exploit those weaknesses.

8.  This exploitation causes great harm to every living thing on Earth.

9.  Fear and anger and guilt were needed for man to survive, but love and joy are needed for man to even exist.

10. No one can find joy in their life by turning control of that life over to those who exploit it. Self love and self discipline are the keystones to everything positive in life, and can only come from self respect.

11. Self respect comes from refusing to believe those who lie to you for your own good, and from refusing to pay blackmail to emotional manipulators. Self respect comes from claiming value for your own life.

12. You are the only one who may bestow upon another the gift of a claim on your time, your energy, your money or your life. No one may ever impose a 'moral' imperative upon another by force.

13. Your life has absolutely **no value** to those who rule you: they waste not a whit of their own energy (while they are rather casual about wasting yours) to protect you or your life. You must defend your own life because no one else will.

14. The gods want only one thing from you: you must mind your own business. As long as you do not interfere with others forcibly, you have the right to insist (with as much force as necessary) that others mind their own concerns and leave you to yours.

15. If your life has no value, give it to the government. If it does hold value for you, defend it for yourself. You are better than they have told you: please take back your own life and enjoy it.

# ～Chapter 2～

1. There is no human being on Earth who can understand even their own self, let alone another. No matter **how** much you learn.

2. Try to forgive yourselves anyway. And keep learning.

3. Forgive yourself, believe in yourself, learn all you can, and enjoy.

4. Be good to each other, and to yourselves. You are all you have.

5. Be responsible, and be free. Live for joy. Love all you can.

6. **And above all else, KYFHO.**

# ~Appendix 1~
# To Start Your Education

The Authors on this list are each individually here for the same two reasons. None of them, we believe, will ever offer you a fact that they do not honestly believe is true; nor will they offer an opinion that is not absolutely their own.

FIRST:

Morgan, Elaine. *The Descent of Woman.* New York: Stein & Day, *1972*

Wilson, F. Paul. *An Enemy of the State.* New York: Doubleday, *1980.*

Heinlein, Robert Anson. *Job: A Comedy of Justice.* New York: Ballentine, *1984*

—*The Moon is a Harsh Mistress.* New York: Putnam, *1966*

Rand, Ayn. *Atlas Shrugged.* New York: Random House, *1957*

And as soon as possible:

Everything else by Heinlein, Rand, Morgan and Wilson

Please make sure to read:

Everything you can find by Robert J. Ringer

Everything you can find by "Adam Smith"
And for health information:
Harvey and Marilyn Diamond
Richard L. Hittleman
If you read these authors, you will start making your
own reading list. Enjoy!

# ∼Appendix 2∼
# For More Information About Livism and Kyfho

The Livism Foundation, Inc. is delighted to share more about Livism, the Science of Living Right, and about the philosophy of KYFHO.

We offer seminars and individual instruction in Livism, from $1000 for a weekend to $1,000,000 for Membership in the Foundation. Applicants must pass a written and oral interview process. Places in classes fill fast; write today to find out how you can qualify.

Please e-mail us at: SaintSierra@aol.com

And we're on the Web at www.saintsierra.com

Or send an S. A. S. E. to

The Livism Foundation, Inc.

P. O. Box 201121

Denver, CO 80220

Hope to hear from you soon!

Make money, stay safe, be happy; and above all else, KYFHO.

Printed in the United States
30575LVS00002B/1

9 780595 001569